BLACK & DECKER

HOME IMPROVEMENT LIBRARY™

Carpentry: Remodeling

Framing & Installing Doors & Windows
Removing & Building Walls

CREATIVE
PUBLISHING
international

MINNETONKA, MINNESOTA

Contents

Why Remodel? **4**
Portfolio of Ideas 6
Project Planning **10**
Anatomy of Your House 11
Window & Door Openings 14
Code Requirements 16
Planning Door
   & Window Installations 18
Drawing Plans
   & Getting a Building Permit 24
Tools & Materials 26

Remodeling Projects **29**
A Remodeling Project
   Step-by-Step 30
Remodeling Basics **34**
Preparing the Work Area 35
Removing Interior Surfaces 38
Removing Old Doors & Windows . 42
Removing Exterior Surfaces 44
Making Temporary Supports 52

Removing & Building Walls **56**
Removing a Wall 58
Building a Partition Wall 62

Copyright © 1992
Creative Publishing International, Inc.
5900 Green Oak Drive
Minnetonka, Minnesota 55343
1-800-328-3895
All rights reserved
Printed in U.S.A.

Books available in this series:
*Everyday Home Repairs, Decorating With
Paint & Wallcovering, Carpentry: Tools •
Shelves • Walls • Doors, Kitchen
Remodeling, Building Decks, Home
Plumbing Projects & Repairs, Basic Wiring &
Electrical Repairs, Workshop Tips &
Techniques, Advanced Home Wiring,
Carpentry: Remodeling, Landscape
Design & Construction, Bathroom
Remodeling, Built-In Projects for the Home,
Kitchen & Bathroom Ideas, Refinishing &
Finishing Wood, Exterior Home Repairs &*

*Improvements, Home Masonry Repairs &
Projects, Building Porches & Patios, Deck &
Landscape Ideas, Flooring Projects &
Techniques, Advanced Deck Building,
Advanced Home Plumbing*

Library of Congress
Cataloging-in-Publication Data

Carpentry: remodeling.

p. cm.—(Black & Decker home
improvement library)
Includes index.
ISBN 0-86573-720-7 (hardcover).
ISBN 0-86573-721-5 (softcover).
1. Carpentry—Amateurs' manuals.
2. Dwellings—Remodeling—Amateurs'
manuals.
I. Cy DeCosse Incorporated.
II. Series.
TH5607.C35 1992   92-16327
694—dc20

President: Iain Macfarlane

CARPENTRY: REMODELING
Created by: The Editors of Creative
Publishing International, Inc., in cooperation
with Black & Decker. **BLACK & DECKER** is a
trademark of the Black & Decker
Corporation and is used under license.

Framing & Installing Doors **66**

Framing a Door Opening 67
Installing an Interior Door 72
Installing an Entry Door 74
Installing a Storm Door 78
Installing a Patio Door 80

Framing & Installing Windows . . . **86**

Installing a Bay Window 94
Installing a Skylight 104

Completing the Project **114**

Finishing the Exterior 115
Finishing Walls & Ceilings 118
Installing Trim Moldings 122
Patching Flooring 124

Index **126**

NOTICE TO READERS

This book provides useful instructions, but we cannot anticipate all of your working conditions or the characteristics of your materials and tools. For safety, you should use caution, care, and good judgment when following the procedures described in this book. Consider your own skill level and the instructions and safety precautions associated with the various tools and materials shown. Neither the publisher nor Black & Decker® can assume responsibility for any damage to property or injury to persons as a result of misuse of the information provided.

The instructions in this book conform to "The Uniform Plumbing Code," "The National Electrical Code Reference Book," and "The Uniform Building Code" current at the time of its original publication. Consult your local Building Department for information on building permits, codes, and other laws as they apply to your project.

Managing Editor: Paul Currie
Editor: Bryan Trandem
Project Manager: Carol Harvatin
Senior Art Director: Tim Himsel
Art Director: Dave Schelitzche
Technical Production Editor: Jim Huntley
Copy Editor: Janice Cauley
Photo Directors: Jim Destiche,
   Christopher Wilson
Shop Supervisors: Phil Juntti, Greg Wallace
Set Builders: Tom Cooper, Earl Lindquist,
   Curtis Lund, Tom Rosch, Glenn Terry,
   Wayne Wendland
*Director of Development Planning &
   Production:* Jim Bindas
Production Manager: Amelia Merz
Production Staff: Adam Esco, Joe Fahey,
   Eva Hanson, Jeff Hickman, Paul Najlis,
   Mike Schauer, Nik Wogstad

Studio Manager: Cathleen Shannon
Assistant Studio Manager: Rena Tassone
Lead Photographer: Mark Macemon
Photographers: Rex Irmen, John
   Lauenstein, Paul Najlis, Mike Parker
Contributing Photographers: Phil Aarrestad,
   Kim Bailey, Paul Englund, Chuck Nields,
   Brad Parker, Marc Scholtes, Mike
   Woodside
Models: Helen Chorolec, Kurt Colby, Greg
   Ebel, Matt Robbey, Gary Sandin, Amira
   Stanford
Set Stylist: Susan Backlund
Contributing Writers & Editors: Greg Breining,
   Mark Johanson, Dick Sternberg
Contributing Manufacturers:
   Cooper Industries; Marvin Windows
Contributing Photography:
   courtesy of Marvin Windows

Printed on American paper by:
   R. R. Donnelley & Sons
02 01 00 99 98 / 6 5 4 3 2

Why Remodel?

Remodeling improves your home and makes it fit your changing needs. You increase the value of your home instead of paying the high cost of building or buying a new one. And you continue to enjoy the security of living right where you are, rather than feeling the major disruptions caused by moving.

A successful home remodeling project satisfies recognized needs or solves specific problems. Many people assume the best way to remodel is by adding a new structural addition to their home, but this is not always the case. Updating your existing structure can change the look and increase the usability of your home just as dramatically.

Once you have defined your home improvement needs, you may be surprised to find that the remodeling solutions involve relatively easy changes to your home. For example, to make a room brighter, improve ventilation, create a better view, and make a bridge between indoor and outdoor living areas, you simply can replace a standard window (inset photo) with a patio door (page opposite).

In most cases, your home improvement solution will fall into one of the following simple remodeling categories.

Remove a wall. Combining two small rooms into one large space by removing an existing wall can fill several needs:
• Create a large space for family activities
• Make an open space for social gatherings
• Build a master bedroom suite

Build a wall. Adding a partition wall to divide a large room is an effective way to create a new private space for a variety of uses:
• Add a new bedroom for a growing family
• Create a quiet home office
• Build a children's playroom
• Make a home workshop
• Finish a basement or attic

Install new windows. With a minimum investment, adding or replacing a window can change the look of your home dramatically:
• Make a small room seem larger by bringing in more sunlight
• Add an egress exit for a bedroom
• Improve your view

Before

• Eliminate draftiness from old windows
• Improve ventilation and reduce cooling costs

Install a new door. Replacing an old door or adding a new door can satisfy many needs:
• Make more efficient use of floor space by changing the location of interior doors
• Link indoor and outdoor living areas and improve your view with a patio door
• Reduce heat loss by replacing an old entry door
• Make your home more inviting to guests
• Make your entry more secure against intruders

Carpentry: Remodeling gives you complete directions for planning and completing any of these common remodeling projects. If you decide that a full-scale room addition is the best solution for your needs, hire a contractor to do the major structural work, then save money by finishing the job yourself.

After

Before

After

Portfolio of Ideas

Put out the welcome mat. The owners of this home replaced their old entry door with a new steel door that keeps out winter chills while creating a warm welcome for guests. (See **Installing an Entry Door**, pages 74 to 77.)

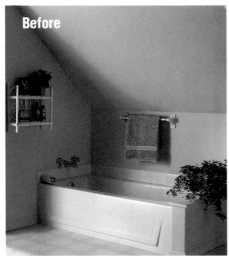

Before

After

See the light. In rooms with limited wall space, skylights are a good way to introduce natural light. In this bathroom with short walls, adding a skylight brightens the room and provides extra ventilation without sacrificing privacy. (See **Installing a Skylight**, pages 104 to 113.)

After

Before

Broaden your horizons. By installing a bay window in place of a double casement window (page 20), the owners of this house brightened their living room and created a sweeping view of a pastoral scene. Bay windows make any room seem larger and brighter, and add visual interest to the exterior of a house. (See **Installing a Bay Window**, pages 94 to 103.)

Before

After

Break down barriers. In this home, the retired owners made a spacious area for family social gatherings by removing a wall and combining small living and dining rooms into a single room. (See **Removing a Wall**, pages 58 to 59.)

(continued next page)

Portfolio of Ideas
(continued)

Brighten a room. Removing a small double-hung window and installing two double casement windows (page 20) was the first step in turning this dark bedroom into a bright space for sitting and relaxing. Casement-style windows were chosen because they provide an unobstructed view and good ventilation. (See **Framing & Installing Windows**, pages 86 to 93).

Before

Find some peace and quiet.
The growing family living in this home added both a children's playroom and a den by building a new partition wall. A sprawling basement room was divided into two smaller, well-defined spaces. (See **Building a Partition Wall**, pages 62 to 65.)

After

Before

Improve traffic flow by relocating a door. In this small room, doors were located in the center of facing walls, causing the foot traffic path to consume most of the usable space. By shifting one of the doors to open into an adjacent hall, the owners turned this wasted space into a functional office. (See **Framing & Installing Doors** pages 66 to 73).

After

After

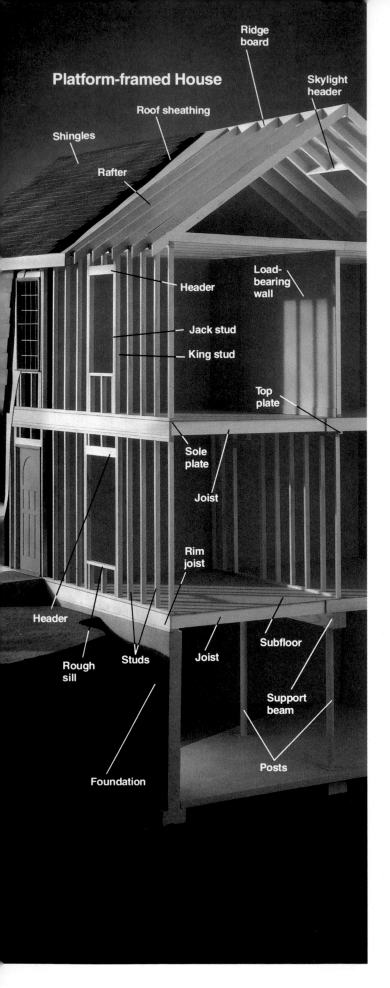

Platform-framed House

- Ridge board
- Skylight header
- Roof sheathing
- Shingles
- Rafter
- Header
- Load-bearing wall
- Jack stud
- King stud
- Top plate
- Sole plate
- Joist
- Rim joist
- Header
- Rough sill
- Studs
- Joist
- Subfloor
- Support beam
- Posts
- Foundation

Project Planning

When planning a remodeling project, you will need to consider and choose from dozens of design and construction options. Making the proper choices helps ensure that your project will increase both your present enjoyment and the future value of your home.

Using professionals: As you plan your remodeling project, consider hiring professionals if you are unsure of your own skills. For example, if you are removing a long load-bearing wall, you may want to hire a builder to install the heavy permanent header, but do all other work yourself. If your project requires changes to the electrical and plumbing systems, you also may want to leave this work to licensed professionals.

Topics covered in this section include:

- The anatomy of your house (pages 11 to 15)
- Code requirements (pages 16 to 17)
- Choosing windows and doors (pages 18 to 23)
- Drawing plans and getting a building permit (pages 24 to 25)
- Tools and materials for remodeling (pages 26 to 27)

Anatomy of a Platform-framed House

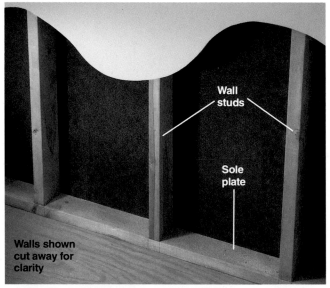

- Wall studs
- Sole plate
- **Walls shown cut away for clarity**

Platform framing (photos, left and above) is identified by the floor-level sole plates and ceiling-level top plates to which the wall studs are attached. Most houses built after 1930 use platform framing. If you do not have access to unfinished areas, you can remove the wall surface at the bottom of a wall to determine what kind of framing was used in your home.

Project Planning
The Anatomy of Your House

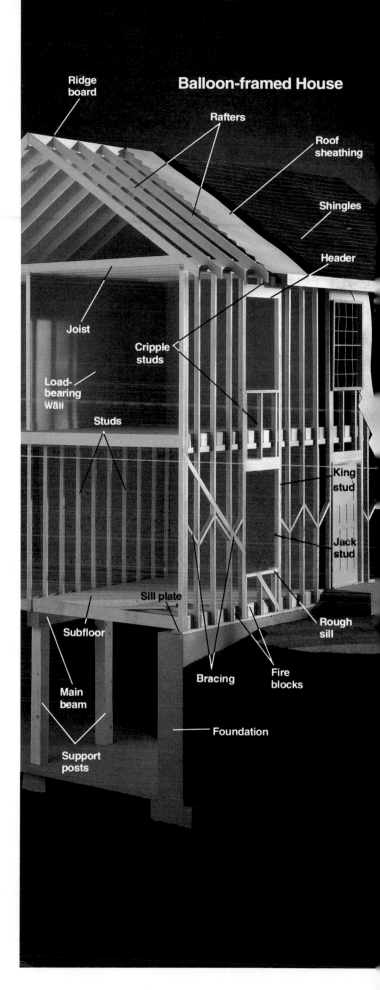

Planning a do-it-yourself remodeling project requires that you understand a few basics of home construction and building terminology. For general reference, use the models shown on these pages while planning your project.

If you plan to modify exterior walls, you must determine if your house was built using platform- or balloon-style framing. The framing style of your home determines what kind of temporary supports you will need to install while the work is in progress. If you have trouble determining what type of framing was used in your home, refer to original blueprints, if you have them, or consult a building contractor or licensed home inspector.

Anatomy of a Balloon-framed House

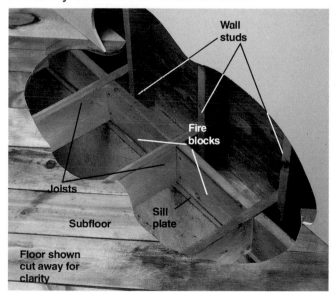

Balloon framing (photos, right and above) is identified by wall studs that run uninterrupted from the roof to a sill plate on the foundation, without the sole plates and top plates found in platform-framed walls (page opposite). Balloon framing was used in houses built before 1930, and is still used in some new home styles, especially those with high vaulted ceilings.

Floor & Ceiling Anatomy

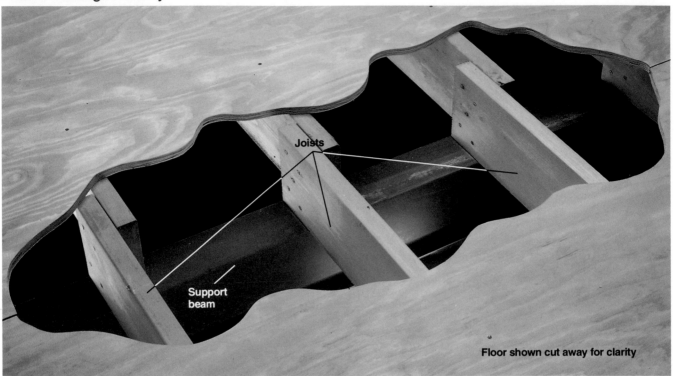

Floor shown cut away for clarity

Joists carry the structural load of floors and ceilings. The ends of the joists are held up by support beams, foundations, or load-bearing walls. Rooms used as living areas must be supported by floor joists that are at least 2 × 8 in size. Floors with smaller joists can be reinforced with "sister" joists (photos, below).

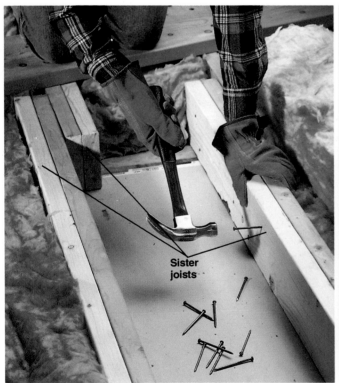

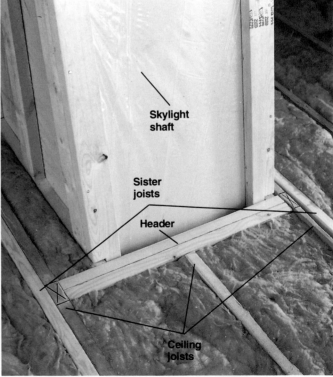

Floors with 2 × 6 joists, like those sometimes found in attics, cannot support living areas unless "sister" joists are attached alongside each original joist to strengthen it (above, left). This often is necessary

when an attic is converted to a living area. Sister joists also are used to help support a header when ceiling joists must be cut, such as when framing a skylight shaft (above, right; and page 104).

Roof Anatomy

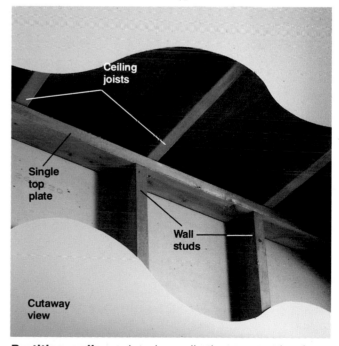

Rafters made from 2 × 4s or 2 × 6s spaced every 16" or 24" are used to support roofs in most houses built before 1950. If necessary, rafters can be cut to make room for a large skylight. Check in your attic to determine if your roof is framed with rafters or roof trusses (right).

Trusses are prefabricated "webs" made from 2" dimension lumber. They are found in many houses built after 1950. Never cut through or alter roof trusses. If you want to install a skylight in a house with roof trusses, buy skylights that fit in the space between the trusses.

Wall Anatomy

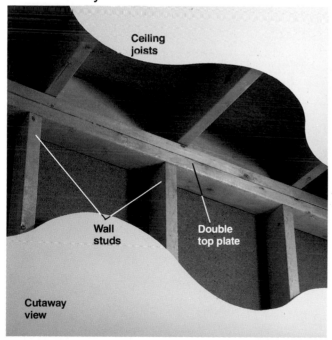

Load-bearing walls carry the structural weight of your home. In platform-framed houses, load-bearing walls can be identified by double top plates made from two layers of framing lumber. Load-bearing walls include all exterior walls, and any interior walls that are aligned above support beams (page 10).

Partition walls are interior walls that are not load-bearing. Partition walls have a single top plate. They can be perpendicular to the floor and ceiling joists but will not be aligned above support beams. Any interior wall that is parallel to floor and ceiling joists is a partition wall.

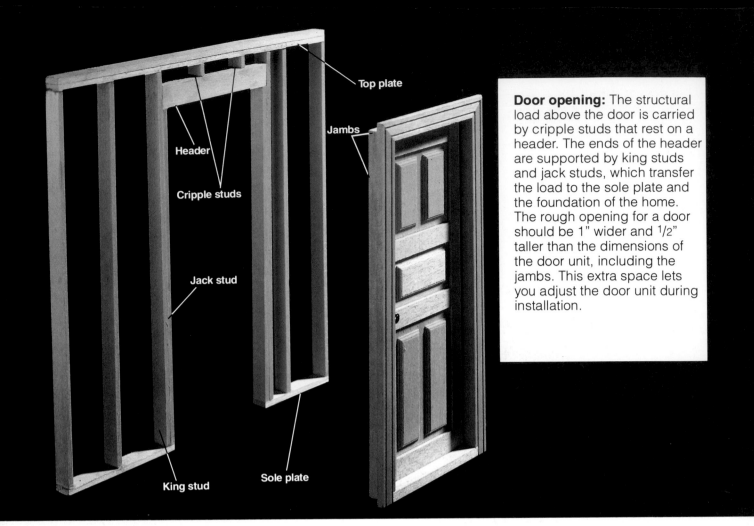

Top plate

Jambs

Header

Cripple studs

Jack stud

King stud

Sole plate

Door opening: The structural load above the door is carried by cripple studs that rest on a header. The ends of the header are supported by king studs and jack studs, which transfer the load to the sole plate and the foundation of the home. The rough opening for a door should be 1" wider and 1/2" taller than the dimensions of the door unit, including the jambs. This extra space lets you adjust the door unit during installation.

Anatomy of Window & Door Openings

Many remodeling projects, like installing new doors or windows, require that you cut one or more studs in a load-bearing wall to create an opening. When planning your project, remember that the wall openings will require a permanent support beam, called a header, to carry the structural load directly above the removed studs.

The required size for the header is set by the Building Code, and varies according to the width of the rough opening. For a window or door opening, a header can be built from two pieces of 2" dimension lumber sandwiched around 3/8" plywood (chart, right). When a large portion of a load-bearing wall (or the entire wall) is removed, a laminated beam product can be used to make the new header (page 57).

If you will be cutting more than one wall stud, make temporary supports to carry the structural load until the header is installed (pages 52 to 55).

Recommended Header Sizes

Rough Opening Width	Recommended Header Construction
Up to 3 ft.	3/8" plywood between two 2 x 4s
3 ft. to 5 ft.	3/8" plywood between two 2 x 6s
5 ft. to 7 ft.	3/8" plywood between two 2 x 8s
7 ft. to 8 ft.	3/8" plywood between two 2 x 10s

Recommended header sizes shown above are suitable for projects where a full story and roof are located above the rough opening. This chart is intended for rough estimating purposes only. For actual requirements, contact an architect or your local building inspector. For spans greater than 8 ft., see page 57.

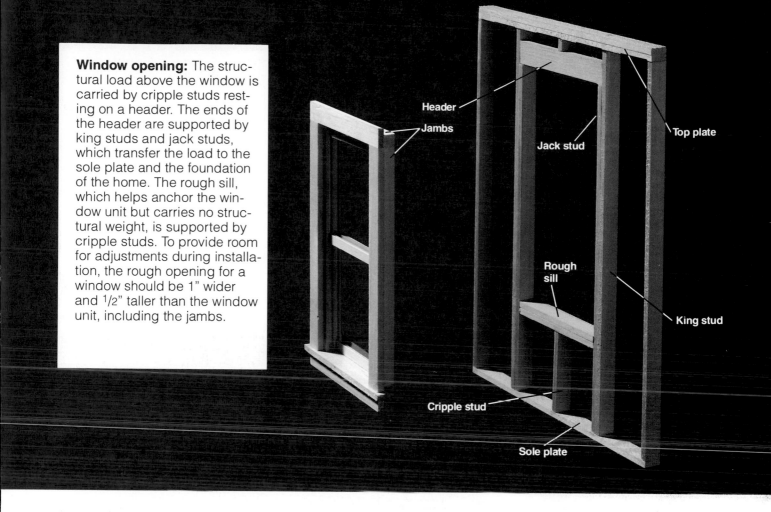

Window opening: The structural load above the window is carried by cripple studs resting on a header. The ends of the header are supported by king studs and jack studs, which transfer the load to the sole plate and the foundation of the home. The rough sill, which helps anchor the window unit but carries no structural weight, is supported by cripple studs. To provide room for adjustments during installation, the rough opening for a window should be 1" wider and 1/2" taller than the window unit, including the jambs.

Header

Jambs

Jack stud

Top plate

Rough sill

King stud

Cripple stud

Sole plate

Framing Options for Window & Door Openings (new lumber shown in yellow)

  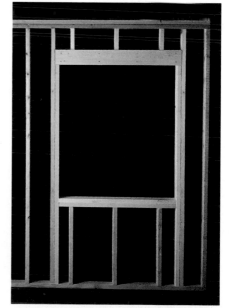

Use an existing opening to avoid new framing work. This is a good option in homes with masonry exteriors, which are difficult to alter. Order a replacement unit that is 1" narrower and 1/2" shorter than the rough opening.

Enlarge an existing opening to simplify the framing work. In many cases you can use an existing king stud and jack stud to form one side of the enlarged opening.

Frame a new opening when installing a window or door where none existed, or when replacing a smaller unit with one that is much larger.

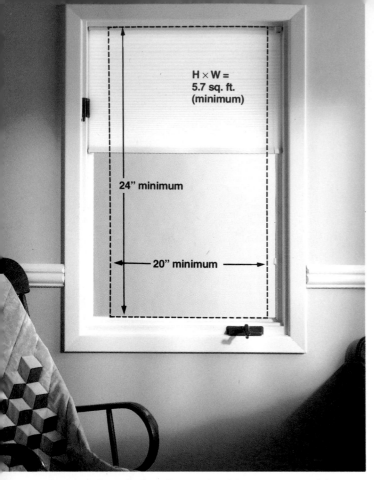

An egress window is required in rooms used for sleeping if there is no other escape route. A window used as an egress should provide an unobstructed opening of 5.7 sq. ft. Height can be no less than 24" and width can be no less than 20". Casement windows offer a large clear opening, making them a good choice for egress installations.

One entry door in a home must have a clear opening at least 32" wide and 6 ft. 8" high. Smaller doors are allowed for secondary entries.

Project Planning
Code Requirements

To ensure safe houses and protect property values, your community requires that all remodeling projects conform to a standard Building Code. Specific codes and standards vary from community to community, but most are based on a model code known as the national Uniform Building Code (UBC). The requirements shown on these pages are from this Code. The UBC contains minimum construction safety standards, and is revised every three years. Copies of the UBC are available at most libraries and bookstores.

Your local building inspector is the best source of information about local Building Codes. Visit or call your inspector early during your planning to find out which parts of the project are subject to local Code, and what you must do to comply. Remember that local Codes vary, and they always

take precedence over the UBC standards. For projects that require changes to the framing members in your home, you always need to get a formal building permit and have your work approved by an official building inspector.

If the inspector feels that strict compliance with the Code would cause an unreasonable restriction to the free use of your property, he may grant you a conditional exemption, called a variance.

If your remodeling project involves changes to the heating, air conditioning, electrical, or plumbing systems, there will be additional code requirements to follow. Most communities require separate work permits and inspections when these systems are altered.

Common Code Requirements for Remodeling Projects

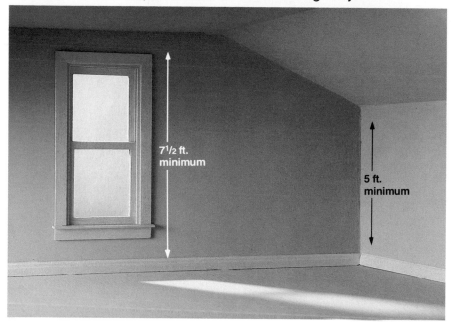

Room Type	Minimum Size
Bedroom	80 sq. ft.
Living room	150 sq. ft.
Family room	110 sq. ft.
Office	64 sq. ft.
Kitchen	50 sq. ft.
Bathroom (full)	35 sq. ft.
Other rooms	70 sq. ft.
Hallway	3 ft. wide

Ceiling height for rooms used as living areas must be at least 7$\frac{1}{2}$ ft. In rooms with sloped ceilings, at least half the floor space must meet minimum ceiling height requirements, and all walls must be at least 5 ft. high. In kitchens, halls, and bathrooms, ceilings must be least 7 ft. high.

Room size recommendations depend on the use of the space, and vary from community to community. Use the chart above as a general reference, but always contact your local building inspector for complete details.

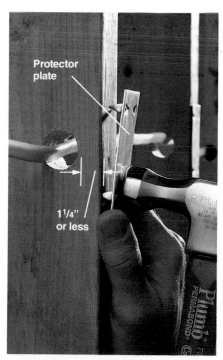

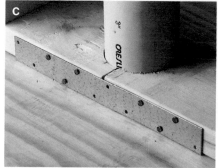

Use protector plates where wires or pipes pass through framing members and are less than 1$\frac{1}{4}$" from the face. The plates prevent wallboard screws or nails from puncturing wires or pipes.

Metal framing connectors may be required in some communities, especially in areas prone to high winds or earthquakes. Metal joist hangers (A), stud ties (B), connector straps (C), and post-and-beam saddles (D) all provide extra reinforcement to structural joints. Wood joints made with metal connectors are stronger than toenailed joints.

Planning Door & Window Installations

Most windows and doors are prehung units designed for easy installation. They are available in a vast range of styles and finishes. The units are preassembled, and trim moldings are either preattached or packed with the unit. Metal hardware is included with all window units, and with some doors. Top-quality windows and doors usually must be special ordered, and require two to four weeks for delivery.

Doors and windows link your home to the outside world and are the most important design elements in any remodeling project. Adding new windows makes your home brighter and makes living spaces feel larger. Replacing a shabby entry door can make your home more inviting to guests and more secure against intruders.

When planning your remodeling project, remember that the choice and placement of doors and windows will affect your life-style. For example, installing a large patio door is a good way to join indoor and outdoor living areas, but it also changes the traffic patterns through your house and affects your personal privacy.

In addition to style, consider the size and placement of windows and doors as you plan the project. Most homeowners install new windows to provide a better view, but remember that a well-positioned window also can reduce heating and cooling bills by serving as a passive solar collector in the cooler months and by improving ventilation in the summer.

Choose new doors and windows that match the style and shape of your home. For traditional home styles, strive for balance when planning windows and doors. In the colonial-style home shown on the left, carefully chosen window units match the scale and proportions of the structure, creating a pleasing symmetry. In the home on the right, mismatched windows conflict with the traditional look of the home.

Tips for Planning Door & Window Installations

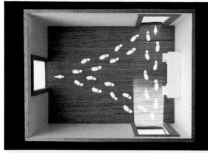

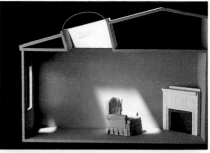

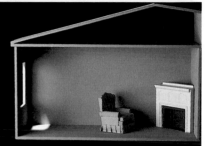

Traffic patterns through the home are determined by the placement of doors. Rooms with many doors seem smaller because traffic patterns consume much of the available space (top). When planning room layout, reserve plenty of space for doors to swing freely.

Divided window panes in windows and patio doors lend a traditional appearance to a home, and help create interesting lighting patterns in a room. Snap-in grills (shown), available for most windows and doors, are an inexpensive way to achieve this effect.

Consider the effect of sunlight when planning window positions. For example, when installing a skylight, choose a location and build a shaft to direct sunlight where you want it.

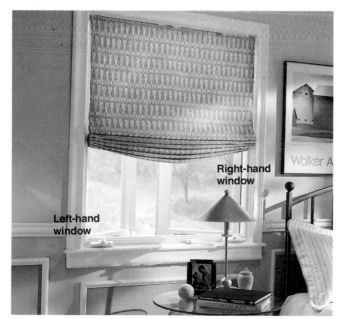

Right-hand window

Left-hand window

Right-hand vs. left-hand: Doors and casement windows are available in both right-hand or left-hand models, and this swing direction must be specified when ordering the units. When opened away from the operator, right-hand units swing to the right, left-hand units to the left. Double window units often have one right-hand and one left-hand unit. If you are installing a single window, choose a model that will catch prevailing breezes when it is opened.

Window combinations can be custom-ordered from the manufacturer. Unusual shapes, like the casement window with attached round top shown here, work well in contemporary-style homes, and also can help create a visual accent in a traditional-style home.

Casement windows pivot on hinges mounted on the side. They are available in many sizes, and in multi-window units that combine as many as five separate windows. Casement windows have a contemporary look, and offer an unobstructed view and good ventilation. They work well as egress windows (page 16).

Double-hung windows slide up and down, and have a traditional appearance. New double-hung windows have a spring-mounted operating mechanism, instead of the troublesome sash weights found on older windows.

Awning windows pivot on hinges mounted at the top. Awning windows work well in combination with other windows, and because they provide ventilation without letting moisture in, they are a good choice in damp climates.

Sliding windows are inexpensive and require little maintenance, but do not provide as much open ventilation as casement windows, since only half of the window can be open at one time.

Skylights introduce extra light into rooms that have limited wall space. Skylights serve as solar collectors on sunny days, and those that also can be opened improve ventilation in the home.

Bay windows make a house feel larger without expensive structural changes. They are available in dozens of sizes and styles.

Door Styles

Interior panel doors have an elegant, traditional look. They are very durable and provide good soundproofing.

Interior hollow-core prehung doors have a contemporary look, and are available in many stock sizes. Hollow-core doors are lightweight and inexpensive.

Decorative storm doors can improve the security, energy efficiency, and appearance of your entry. A storm door prolongs the life of an expensive entry door by protecting it from the elements.

Entry doors with sidelights brighten a dark entry hall, and give an inviting look to your home. In better models, sidelights contain tempered, double-pane glass for better security and energy efficiency.

Sliding patio doors offer good visibility and lighting. Because they slide on tracks and require no floor space for operation, sliding doors are a good choice for cramped spaces where swinging doors do not fit.

French patio doors have an elegant appearance. Weathertight models are used to join indoor and outdoor living areas, while indoor models are used to link two rooms. Because they open on hinges, your room design must allow space for the doors to swing.

Tips for Choosing Doors & Windows

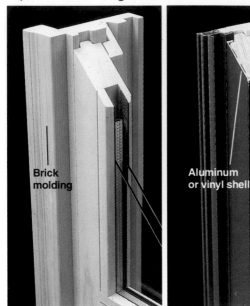

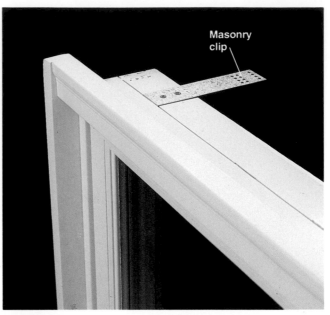

Wood-frames (left) are a good choice for windows and patio doors used in remodeling projects. Their preattached exterior brick moldings blend well with the look of existing windows. **Clad-frame** windows and doors (right) feature an aluminum or vinyl shell. They are used most frequently in new construction, and are attached with nailing flanges (page 115) that fit underneath the siding material.

Polymer coatings are optional on some wood-frame windows and doors. Polymer-coated windows and doors are available in a variety of colors, and do not need painting. To avoid using casing nails, which would pierce the weatherproof coating, you can anchor polymer-coated units with masonry clips that are screwed to the jambs and to the interior framing members (page 93).

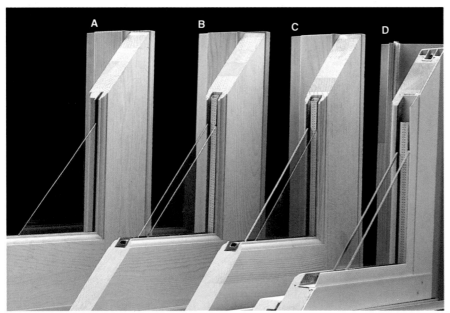

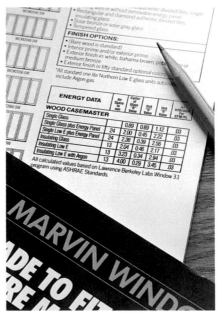

Several types of glass are available from window and door manufacturers. Single-pane glass (A) is suitable only in very mild climates. Double-pane (B) have a sealed air space between the layers of glass to reduce heat loss. They are available in several variations with improved insulating ability, including "low-E" glass with an invisible coating of metal on one surface, and gas-filled windows containing an inert gas, like argon. In southern climates, double-glazed tinted glass (C) reduces heat buildup. Tempered glass (D) has extra strength for use in patio doors and large picture windows.

R-values of windows and doors, listed in manufacturers' catalogs, indicate the energy efficiency of the unit. Higher R-values indicate better insulating properties. Top-quality windows can have an R-value as high as 4.0. Exterior doors with R-values above 10 are considered energy-efficient.

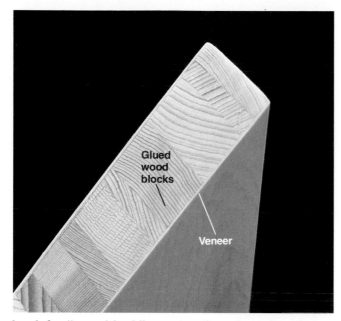

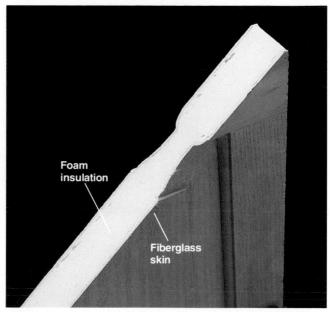

Look for "core-block" construction when choosing exterior wooden doors. Core-block doors are made from layers of glued or laminated wood blocks covered with a veneer. Because the direction of the wood grain alternates, core-block doors are less likely to warp than solid-core doors.

Fiberglass doors are expensive, but they are sturdy, have excellent insulating values, and require little maintenance. The fiberglass surface is designed to have the texture of wood and can be stained or painted different colors.

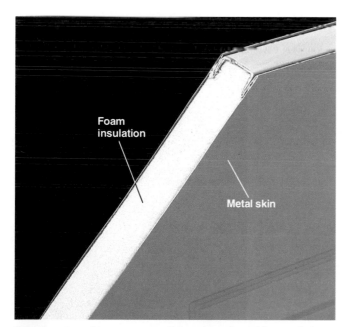

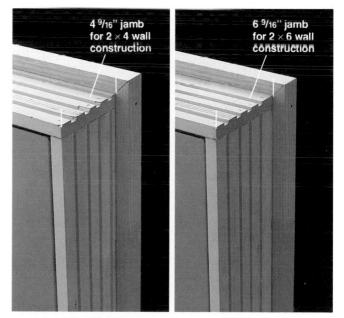

Steel entry doors are well insulated and have tight-fitting magnetic weather seals. Steel doors are less expensive than wooden doors and require little maintenance.

Check wall thickness before ordering doors and windows. Manufacturers will customize the frame jambs to match whatever wall construction you have. Find your wall thickness by measuring the jamb width on an existing door or window.

Inexpensive computer software designed for the home remodeler can help create a floor plan for your project. Many public libraries have computers and software available for use, and some building centers provide computer-assisted design services to their customers.

Project Planning

Drawing Plans & Getting a Building Permit

Any remodeling project that includes additions or changes to the home structure requires a building permit from your local building inspector. Before beginning any project, always contact your inspector to find out if you need a permit. If your project includes changes to mechanical systems, like the wiring or plumbing, you will need additional permits for this work.

To obtain a building permit, you must have a floor plan, elevation drawing, and a materials list to show to the inspector. You also must pay a small permit fee. The amount of the fee depends on the estimated cost of your project.

When the inspector issues the work permit, you also will receive a schedule for the required on-site inspections. For most projects, the inspector will visit your site after the framing work is done, but before the walls are finished.

How to Draw Plans

1 Use existing blueprints of your home, if available, to trace original floor plans and elevation drawings onto white paper. Copy the measurement scale of the original blueprints onto the traced drawings. Make photocopies of the traced drawings, then use the photocopies to experiment with remodeling ideas. Test your ideas in the project area (top photo, page opposite).

How to Test Remodeling Ideas

couch

Plot possible locations for new windows and doors with masking tape. Always mark the full swinging arc of hinged doors. Use newspaper or cardboard to make full-size cutouts of furniture, and use them to experiment with different room layouts. Designers recommend that your floor plan allow ample room around furniture: 22" around a bed; 36" around couches, chairs, and tables; 40" in front of dressers, chests, and closets. Walk through the room along different paths to judge how the room elements will interact. Remember to allow a 40"-wide path for foot traffic across a room. Once you have found a pleasing layout, make final floor plan and elevation drawings (below).

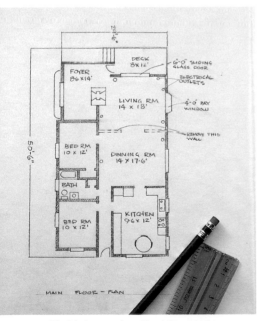

2 Make a detailed floor plan showing the layout of the area that will be remodeled, including accurate measurements. Show the location of new and existing doors and windows, wiring, and plumbing fixtures.

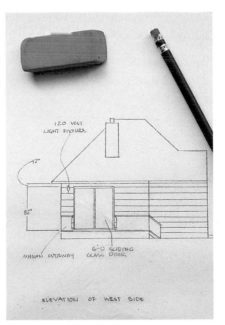

3 Make elevation drawings showing the side view layout of windows and doors, as viewed from both inside and outside the home. Indicate the size of windows and doors, ceiling heights, and the location of wiring and plumbing fixtures.

4 Create a complete list showing the materials you intend to use. The list will help the inspector determine if the materials meet accepted standards for strength and fire resistance, and will help you estimate the cost of the project.

Project Planning
Tools & Materials

In addition to basic carpentry items, your remodeling project probably will require some of the specialty tools and materials shown in these photos. Whenever you are using a new tool, practice your skills on scrap materials.

Before starting, you should be familiar with common hand tools, power tools, and lumber products used in basic carpentry work. These tools and materials are listed in the chart below. A good book on carpentry skills, such as Black & Decker® Home Improvement Library's™ *Carpentry: Tools • Shelves • Walls • Doors*, will show you the basic principles of tool use.

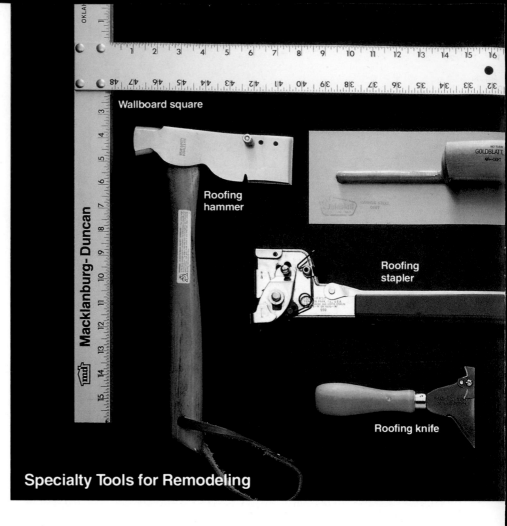

Specialty Tools for Remodeling

Basic Tools & Materials

Hand tools:
- Carpenter's level
- Caulk gun
- Chalk line
- Channel-type pliers
- Combination square
- Coping saw
- Hammer
- Framing square
- Handsaw
- Metal snips
- Pencils/pens
- Plumb bob
- Pry bars
- Ratchet wrench
- Screwdrivers
- Stapler
- Tape measure
- Utility knife
- Wallboard taping knives
- Wheelbarrow
- Wood chisel
- Work belt
- Workmate® bench

Power tools:
- Circular saw
- Cordless screwdrivers
- Drill & bits
- Miter saw

Materials:
- 2" framing lumber
- Common nails
- Drop cloths
- Fiberglass insulation
- Masking tape
- Neon circuit tester
- Plywood
- Shingles
- Siding
- Trim moldings
- Wallboard
- Wallboard compound
- Wallboard tape
- Wood shims
- Wood screws

Materials for Remodeling

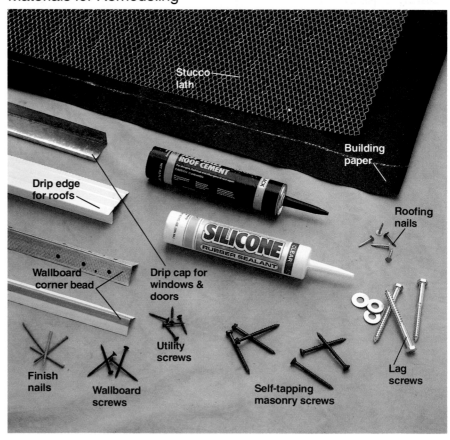

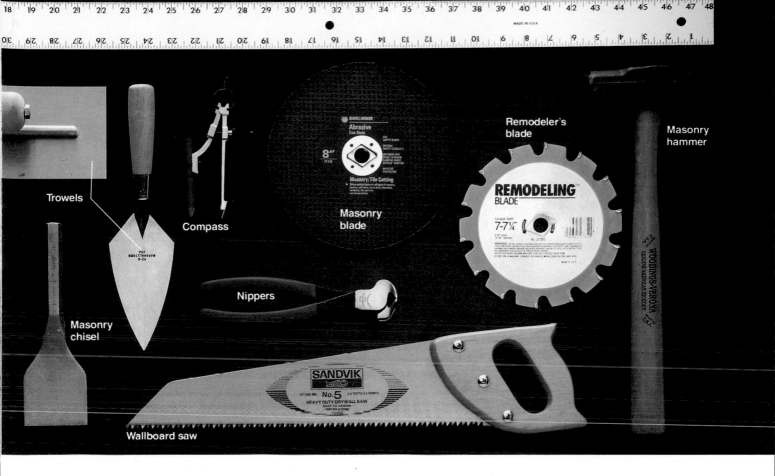

Trowels

Compass

Masonry blade

Remodeler's blade

Masonry hammer

REMODELING BLADE
7-7¼"

Masonry chisel

Nippers

SANDVIK
No.5
HEAVY DUTY DRYWALL SAW

Wallboard saw

Safety Equipment

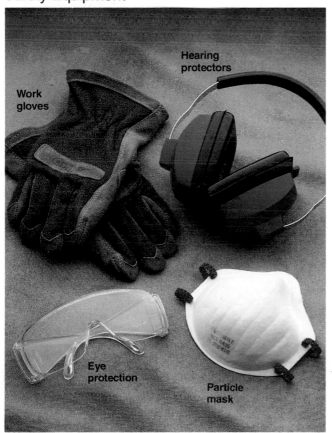

Hearing protectors

Work gloves

Eye protection

Particle mask

Tools You Can Rent

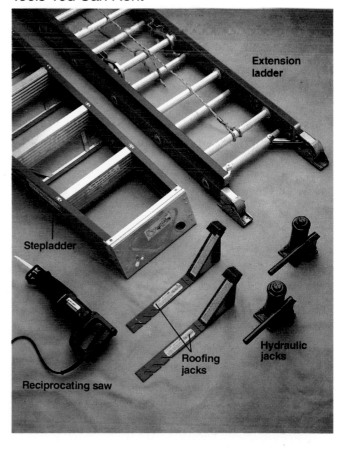

Extension ladder

Stepladder

Reciprocating saw

Roofing jacks

Hydraulic jacks

After

Before

Remodeling Projects

A Remodeling Project Step-by-Step

On the following few pages (30 to 33), you will find a step-by-step overview of a major home remodeling project. Individual projects differ greatly, but most jobs can be organized into these basic steps.

A common mistake made by homeowners is underestimating the project costs and work time. Shop carefully to secure the best prices on materials, and be realistic when estimating the time it will take to complete the job.

Many homeowners budget both their money and time by dividing a large project into separate stages that can be done over a period of months or even years. For example, you might choose to remove an interior wall and install a bay window one summer, then add a skylight and patio door later. If you work in stages, first create a master plan to ensure that each step fits into your overall design.

A Planning Checklist: Before you begin hands-on work, make sure you can answer YES to the following questions:

❑ Do you have a working floor plan and elevation drawings for your project?

❑ Have you made a complete materials list and estimated the job costs?

❑ Do you have the required work permits, and are they displayed properly?

❑ Have you ordered all materials you will need, including window and door units?

❑ Have you scheduled your time realistically and arranged for helpers, if needed?

❑ Have you made provisions for removing demolition materials?

❑ Have you arranged for upgrades to the wiring and plumbing systems?

❑ Do you have the necessary tools and rental equipment?

1 Prepare the work area (pages 35 to 37). Remove trim moldings, and shut off power and plumbing to the wall areas that will be altered. Remove coverplates from the switches, receptacles, and heating ducts in the project area. Protect the floors with drop cloths, and cover doors leading to other areas of the house with plastic to confine dust to the remodeling area.

2 Remove interior surfaces (pages 38 to 41). Mark rough openings for the new doors and windows, then remove the interior wall surfaces. Make sure to remove enough wall surface to provide easy access for installing new framing members. After removing wall surfaces, remove old door and window units (pages 42 to 43). Clear away all trash before continuing with your project.

3 Make temporary supports (pages 52 to 55) if your project requires you to cut more than one stud in a load-bearing wall. Temporary supports help brace the upper structure of your home until the framing work is done. Load-bearing walls include all exterior walls, and most interior walls that run perpendicular to floor joists. Interior walls running parallel to joists are non-load-bearing (partition) walls, and do not require temporary supports.

Temporary support

(continued next page)

Non-load-bearing wall

4 Remove and build walls (pages 58 to 65). If you are removing an interior non-load-bearing wall, simply remove the wall surfaces and cut away the studs. However, if you are removing a load-bearing wall, you must make temporary supports and replace the wall with a sturdy permanent header and posts to support the weight previously carried by the removed wall.

5 Frame the openings for the doors (pages 66 to 71) and windows (pages 86 to 89). After the framing work is complete, remove the exterior surfaces (pages 44 to 49) and install the door and window units.

6 Install doors (pages 72 to 85) and windows (pages 90 to 113). Complete the exterior finishing work as soon as possible to protect the wall cavities against moisture.

7 Complete the project (pages 114 to 125). First patch and paint the exterior siding and attach any required exterior moldings. When completing the interior work, install the wallboard first, then paint or attach wallcovering. Finally, patch the floors, and install the wood trim moldings.

Remodeling Basics

Most remodeling projects share the same basic preparation techniques and follow a similar sequence. Organizing your project into stages helps you work efficiently and lets you break large projects into a series of weekend jobs.

During the demolition phase, try to salvage or recycle materials wherever possible. Window and door units, molding, carpeting, electrical and plumbing fixtures that are in good shape can be used elsewhere or sold to salvage yards. Most raw metals are accepted at recycling centers. Wallboard and insulation seldom are worth salvaging.

If your project requires a permit from the local building inspector, do not begin work until the inspector has approved your plans and issued the permit. Display the permit sticker on a window or outer wall so it is visible from the street. If your project requires plumbing or electrical work, additional permits are needed.

Information in this section:

- Preparing the work area (pages 35 to 37)
- Removing interior surfaces (pages 38 to 41)
- Removing old doors and windows (pages 42 to 43)
- Removing exterior surfaces (pages 44 to 51)
- Making temporary supports when cutting studs (pages 52 to 55)

Preparing the Work Area

Good preparation of the work area shortens work time, simplifies cleanup, and protects the rest of your house from dirt and damage.

A job site cluttered with old nails, boards, and other materials poses a safety hazard, so take the time to clear away the trash whenever materials begin to pile up. For large jobs, rent a dumpster to hold the demolition debris.

Many remodeling jobs require that you shut off and reroute electrical wiring, plumbing pipes, and other utility lines that run through the walls. If you are not comfortable doing this work yourself, hire a professional.

Everything You Need:

Tools: screwdrivers, broom, trash containers, neon circuit tester, electronic stud finder, flat pry bar, channel-type pliers.

Materials: drop cloths, masking tape, building paper, plywood.

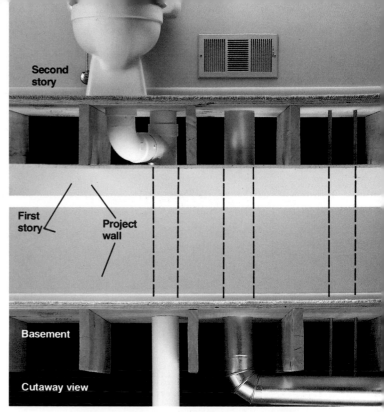

Check for hidden plumbing lines, ductwork, and gas pipes before you cut into a wall. To determine the location of the pipes and ducts, examine the areas directly below and above the project wall. In most cases, pipes, utility lines, and ductwork run through the wall vertically between floors. Original blueprints for your house, if available, usually show the location of the utility lines.

Preparation Tips

Disconnect electrical wiring before you cut into walls. Trace the wiring back to a fixture outside the cutout area, then shut off the power and disconnect the wires leading into the cutout area. Turn the power back on and test for current before cutting into the walls.

Shovel debris through a convenient window into a wheelbarrow to speed up demolition work. Use sheets of plywood to cover shrubs and flower gardens next to open windows and doors. Cover adjoining lawn areas with sheets of plastic or canvas to simplify cleanup.

How to Prepare the Project Area

1 Locate framing members in wall and ceiling areas where you will be working, using an electronic stud finder.

2 Verify the locations of framing members by driving finishing nails through the wall. Mark the studs every 2 ft. from floor to ceiling.

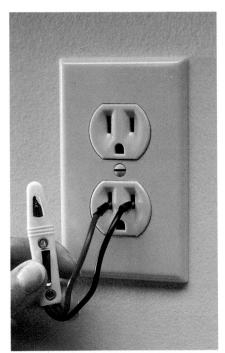

3 Shut off or disconnect the power to electrical fixtures in the wall and ceiling areas where you will be working. Check for power at each fixture, using a neon circuit tester.

4 Shut off the water supply at the main shutoff valve if you are working on wall areas that contain water supply pipes.

5 Remove coverplates from electrical fixtures inside the wall area that will be removed. Tape the mounting screws to the coverplates, and store them in a safe location.

6 Tape dropcloths over doors and heating/air-conditioning ducts to keep demolition dust from circulating through the house. Cover the floors with cardboard and drop cloths to shield them from dust and damage.

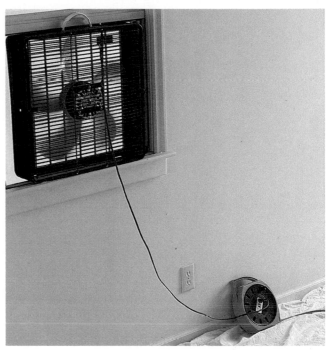

7 Provide ventilation by placing fans in opened windows in the project area. If you have shut off the power, run heavy-duty extension cords from other parts of the house to provide electricity.

8 Loosen trim moldings by prying them up with a flat pry bar. Use a wood block to prevent the pry bar from damaging the wall. When the entire length of molding is loose, separate it from the wall. Be careful when removing trim moldings that will be reused or salvaged: old moldings are brittle and break easily. Label any pieces that will be reused.

9 Remove the nails after you remove each piece of trim molding. To avoid splintering, use a channel-type pliers or nail puller to pull the nails through from the back side of the trim.

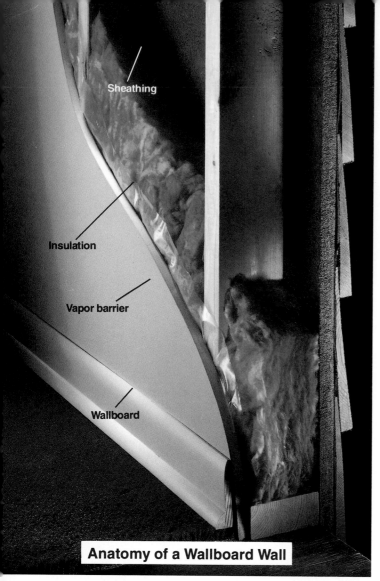

Sheathing

Insulation

Vapor barrier

Wallboard

Anatomy of a Wallboard Wall

Removing Interior Surfaces

You must remove interior wall surfaces before you can do the framing work for most remodeling projects. Remove enough surface so there is plenty of room to install the new framing members. When installing a window or door, remove the wall surface from floor to ceiling and all the way to the first wall studs beyond either side of the planned rough opening.

If you have wood paneling, remove it in full sheets if you intend to reuse it. It may be difficult to find new paneling to match the style of your old paneling.

Removing Wallboard

Demolishing a section of wallboard is a messy job, but it is not difficult. If your wallboard was attached with construction adhesive, use a rasp or old chisel to remove the dried adhesive and create a flat surface on the framing members.

Everything You Need:

Tools: tape measure, pencil, stud finder, chalk line, circular saw with remodeler's blade, utility knife, pry bar, eye protection, hammer.

How to Mark Interior Surfaces for Removal

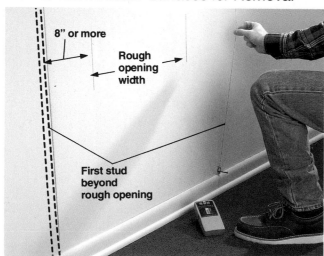

8" or more

Rough opening width

First stud beyond rough opening

Mark the width of the rough opening on the wall, then locate the first stud beyond either side of the planned rough opening. **If the rough opening is more than 8" from the next stud,** use a chalk line to mark a cutting line on the inside edge of the stud. An extra nailing stud will be attached to provide a surface for anchoring wallboard (page 118).

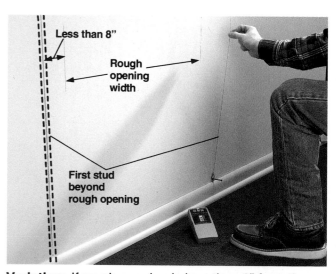

Less than 8"

Rough opening width

First stud beyond rough opening

Variation: If rough opening is less than 8" from the next stud, you will not have room to attach an extra nailing stud. Use a chalk line to mark the cutting line down the center of the wall stud. The exposed portion of the stud will provide a surface for attaching new wallboard when finishing the room.

How to Remove Wallboard

1 Remove the baseboards and other trim, and prepare the work area (pages 35 to 37). Make a 3/4"-deep cut from floor to ceiling along both cutting lines, using a circular saw. Use a utility knife to finish the cuts at the top and bottom, and to cut through the taped horizontal seam where the wall meets the ceiling surface.

2 Insert the end of a pry bar into the cut near a corner of the opening. Pull the pry bar until the wallboard breaks, then tear away the broken pieces. Take care to avoid damaging wallboard outside the project area.

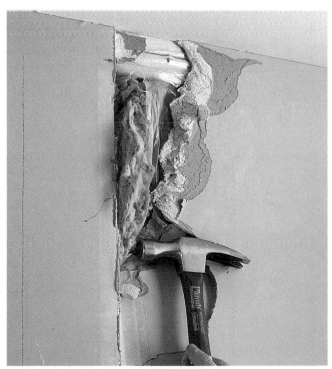

3 Continue removing wallboard by striking the surface with the side of a hammer, then pulling it away from the wall with the pry bar or your hands.

4 Remove nails, screws, and any remaining wallboard from the framing members, using a pry bar. Remove any vapor barrier and insulation.

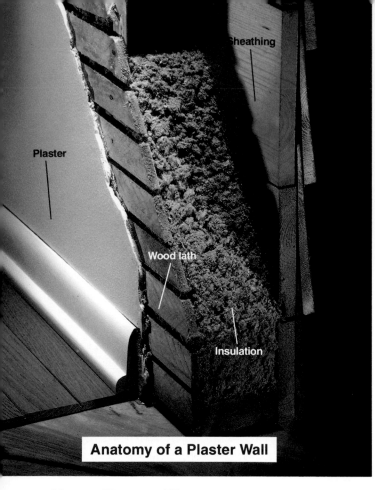

Plaster

Sheathing

Wood lath

Insulation

Anatomy of a Plaster Wall

Removing Plaster

Plaster removal is a dusty job, so always wear eye protection and a particle mask during demolition, and use sheets of plastic to protect furniture and to block open doorways. Plaster walls are very brittle, so work carefully to avoid cracking the plaster in areas that will not be removed.

If the material being removed is most of the wall surface, consider removing the whole interior surface of the wall. Replacing the entire wall with wallboard is easier and produces better results than trying to patch around the project area.

Everything You Need:

Tools: straightedge, pencil, chalk line, utility knife, eye protection, particle mask, work gloves, hammer, pry bar, reciprocating saw or jig saw, metal snips.

Materials: masking tape, scrap piece of 2 × 4.

How to Remove Plaster

1 Mark the wall area to be removed by following the directions on page 38. Apply a double layer of masking tape along the outside edge of each cutting line.

2 Score each line several times with a utility knife, using a straightedge as a guide. Scored lines should be at least 1/8" deep.

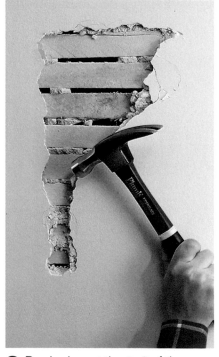

3 Beginning at the top of the wall in the center of the planned opening, break up the plaster by striking the wall lightly with the side of a hammer. Clear away all plaster from floor to ceiling to within 3" of the lines.

4 Break the plaster along the edges by holding a scrap piece of 2 × 4 on edge just inside the scored line, and rapping it with a hammer. Use a pry bar to remove the remaining plaster.

5 Shut off power and examine the wall for wiring and plumbing. Cut through the lath along the edges of the plaster, using a reciprocating saw or jig saw.

Metal lath

Variation: If the wall has metal lath laid over the wood lath, use a metal snips to clip the edges of the metal lath. Press the jagged edges of the lath flat against the stud. The cut edges of metal lath are very sharp, so be sure to wear work gloves.

6 Remove the lath from the studs, using a pry bar. Pry away any remaining nails, and remove any vapor barrier and insulation.

Masking tape used to keep glass from shattering.

Project Basics
Removing Old Doors & Windows

If your remodeling project requires removing old doors and windows, do not start this work until all preparation work is finished and the interior wall surfaces and trim have been removed. You will want to close up the wall openings as soon as possible, so make sure you have all the tools, framing lumber, and new window and door units you will need before starting the final stages of demolition. Be prepared to finish the work as quickly as possible.

Doors and windows are removed using the same basic procedures. In many cases, the old units can be salvaged for resale or later use, so use care when removing them.

Everything You Need:

Tools: utility knife, flat pry bar, screwdriver, hammer, reciprocating saw.

Materials: plywood sheets.

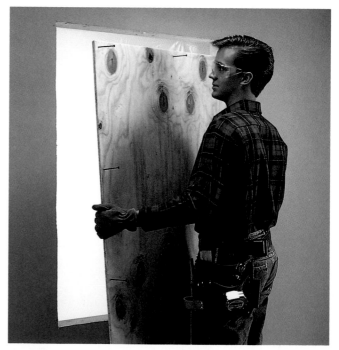

If wall openings cannot be filled immediately, protect your home by covering the openings with scrap pieces of plywood screwed to the framing members. Plastic sheeting stapled to the outside of the openings will prevent moisture damage.

How to Remove Old Windows & Doors

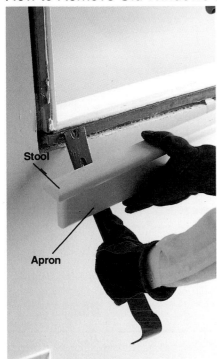

Stool

Apron

1 Pry off the window aprons and stools, using a pry bar.

Sash weight

2 For double-hung windows with sash weights, remove the weights by cutting the cords and pulling the weights from pockets.

3 Cut through the nails holding the window and door frames to the framing members, using a reciprocating saw.

4 Pry the outside brick moldings free from the framing members, using a pry bar.

5 Pull the unit from the rough opening, using a pry bar.

Nailing fin

Variation: For windows and doors attached with nailing fins, cut or pry loose the siding material or brick moldings, then remove the mounting nails holding the unit to the sheathing.

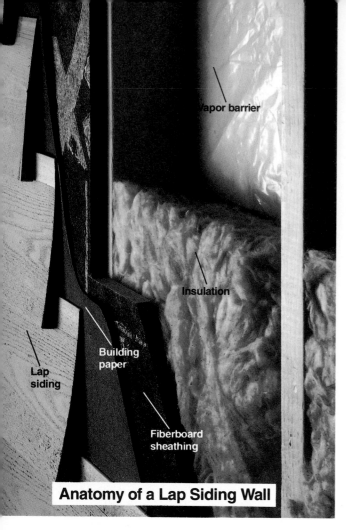

Vapor barrier

Insulation

Building
paper

Lap
siding

Fiberboard
sheathing

Anatomy of a Lap Siding Wall

Removing Exterior Surfaces

Do not remove exterior surfaces until the interior surfaces have been removed and the opening is framed. To protect wall cavities against moisture, install windows or doors as soon as you remove the exterior surfaces.

Working with a brick facade is difficult. You can do the interior framing work yourself, but hire a professional to remove and patch the brickwork.

Removing Siding

Exterior lap siding comes in many types. All are removed using the same basic method, but some materials require specialty saw blades (page 26).

> **Everything You Need:**
>
> Tools: drill with 3/16" × 8" bit, hammer, tape measure, chalk line, circular saw with remodeler's blade, reciprocating saw, eye protection.
>
> Materials: 8d casing nails, straight 1 × 4.

How to Remove Siding

1 From inside, drill through the wall at the corners of the framed opening. Push casing nails through the holes to mark their location. For round-top windows, drill several holes around the curved outline (page 90).

2 Measure the distance between the nails on the outside of the wall to make sure the dimensions are accurate. Mark the cutting lines with a chalk line stretched between the nails. Push the nails back through the wall.

3 Nail a straight 1 × 4 flush against inside edge of right cutting line. Drive nail heads slightly under wood surface with a nail set to prevent scratches to the saw foot. Set circular saw to maximum blade depth.

4 Rest the saw on the 1 × 4, and cut along the marked line, using the edge of the board as a guide. Stop the cuts about 1" short of the corners to keep from damaging the framing members.

5 Reposition the 1 × 4, and make the remaining straight cuts. Drive nails within 1½" of the edge of the board, because the siding under this area will be removed to make room for door or window brick moldings.

Variation: For round-top windows, make curved cuts using a reciprocating saw or jig saw. Move the saw slowly to ensure smooth, straight cuts. To draw an outline for rount-top windows, use a cardboard template (page 89).

6 Complete the cuts at the corner with a reciprocating saw or jig saw.

7 Remove the cut wall section. If you are working with metal siding, wear work gloves. If you wish, remove the siding pieces from the sheathing and save them for future use.

Metal lath

Insulation

Building paper

Stucco layers

Sheathing

Anatomy of a Stucco Wall

Removing Stucco

Stucco is a very hard wall material requiring special cutting tools designed for masonry. Wear safety equipment when doing the cutting.

Repaired areas are difficult to blend into existing stucco, so take care to make accurate, smooth cuts.

Everything You Need:

Tools: drill with 3/16" × 8" twist and masonry bits, tape measure, chalk line, compass, masonry chisel, masonry hammer, eye and hearing protection, circular saw and blades (masonry-cutting and remodeler's), masonry chisels, pry bar.

Materials: 8d casing nails.

How to Remove Stucco

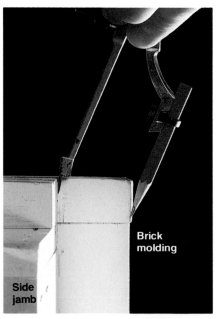

Brick molding

Side jamb

1 From inside, drill through the wall at the corners of the framed opening. Use a twist bit to drill through the sheathing, then change to a masonry bit to finish the holes. Push casing nails through the holes to mark their locations.

2 On the outside wall, measure distances between the nails to make sure the rough opening dimensions are accurate. Mark cutting lines between the nails, using a chalk line.

3 Spread the legs of a compass to match the distance between the side jambs and the edge of the brick molding on the window or door.

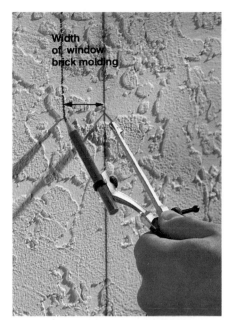

Width of window brick molding

4 Scribe a cutting line on the stucco by moving the compass along the outline, with the compass point held on the marked line. This added margin will allow the window brick molding to fit tight against the wall sheathing.

5 Score the stucco surface around the outside edge of the scribed line, using a masonry chisel and masonry hammer. The scored grooves should be at least 1/8" deep to serve as a guide for the circular saw blade.

6 Make straight cuts using a circular saw and masonry-cutting blade. Make several passes with the saw, gradually deepening cuts until blade just cuts through the metal lath, causing sparks to fly. Stop cuts just before the corners to avoid damaging the stucco past the cutting line, then complete the cuts with a masonry chisel.

Variation: For round-top windows, mark the outline on the stucco, using a cardboard template (page 89), then drill a series of holes around the outline, using a masonry bit. Complete the cut with a masonry chisel.

7 Break up the stucco with a masonry hammer or sledgehammer, exposing the underlying metal lath. Use metal snips to cut through the lath around the opening. Use a pry bar to pull away the lath and attached stucco.

8 Outline the rough opening on the sheathing, using a straightedge as a guide. Cut the rough opening along the inside edge of the framing members, using a circular saw or reciprocating saw (steps 4 and 5, page 45). Remove the cut section of sheathing.

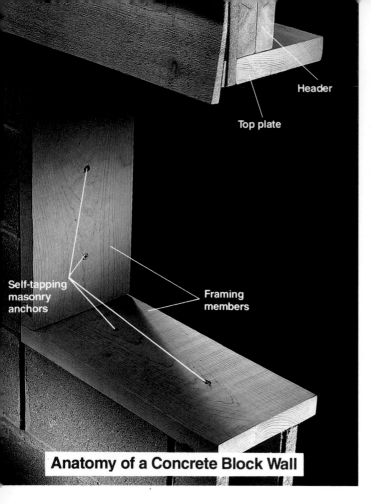

Header

Top plate

Self-tapping masonry anchors

Framing members

Anatomy of a Concrete Block Wall

Removing Concrete Block

Making a new opening in a concrete wall is complicated and can cause damage to your house structure, so leave this work to a professional. However, you can extend an existing opening downward, so long as you leave the load-bearing header intact.

For example, if you have an exposed basement, you can remove an existing picture window and extend the opening in order to install a patio door leading to the back yard. Or, you can extend a small existing window opening to provide an egress window—a Building Code requirement for any sleeping room (page 16).

Everything You Need:

Tools: level, pencil, circular saw with masonry blade, masonry chisel, masonry hammer, eye protection, work gloves, hearing protectors, caulk gun, trowel, drill with 3/16" masonry bit.

Materials: premixed dry concrete, construction adhesive, 2" pressure-treated lumber, self-tapping masonry anchors.

How to Remove Concrete Block

1 Remove old window unit and frame, then mark the rough opening on both the interior and exterior sides of the wall, using a level as a guide.

2 Score the cutting lines, using a masonry chisel and masonry hammer, wearing eye protection and work gloves.

3 Cut along the scored lines with a circular saw and masonry blade. Make many passes with the saw, gradually deepening the cut until the saw blade is at maximum depth.

4 Break both the inside and outside mortar lines on all sides of the center block in the top row of blocks being removed. Use a masonry chisel and hammer.

5 Strike the face of the center block with a masonry hammer until the block either dislodges or breaks into pieces.

6 Chip out large pieces with a masonry chisel. Break mortar around remaining blocks, then chip them out with the masonry chisel and hammer.

How to Frame a Rough Opening in Concrete Block

1 When all blocks are removed, create a smooth surface by filling the hollow areas in the cut blocks with scrap pieces of concrete block, then troweling fresh concrete over the surfaces. Make sure surfaces are flat, then let concrete dry overnight.

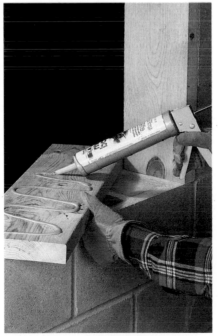

2 Install 2" pressure-treated lumber to frame the opening, using construction adhesive. If the interior wall is finished, size the framing members so they are flush with any existing studs or furring strips.

3 Anchor framing members by drilling pilot holes with a 3/16" masonry bit, then driving self-tapping masonry anchors into the blocks, spaced every 10".

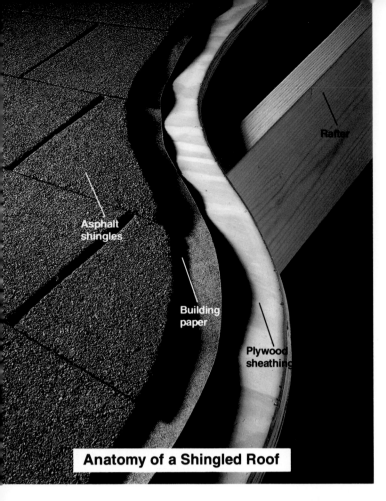

Asphalt shingles

Building paper

Rafter

Plywood sheathing

Anatomy of a Shingled Roof

Removing a Shingled Roof Section

When installing a skylight, you will need to remove a section of roof. Asphalt or fiberglass shingles are easy to remove; but slate, tile, or wood-shingle roofs should be left to a professional.

Use extreme caution whenever you are working on a roof. Never work on a roof alone, and always wear long pants and rubber-soled shoes. Use metal roofing jacks and 2 × 10s to provide a foot rest below the work area (page opposite). If possible, start your roofing project on a calm, clear day when the temperature is between 50° and 70°F. Cold shingles are slippery from condensation, and warm shingles are easily damaged.

Everything You Need:

Tools: ladder, hammer, chalk line, tape measure, roofing jacks, circular saw with old remodeler's blade.

Materials: 8d casing nails, 2 × 4, straight 1 × 4, roofing cement.

How to Remove a Shingled Roof Section

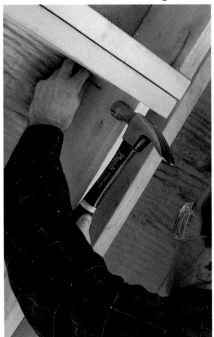

1 After framing the rough opening from the inside (pages 106 to 107), mark the rough opening by driving 8d casing nails through the interior roof sheathing at the corners of the frame.

2 Nail a 2 × 4 diagonally across the framed opening to keep the roof section from falling through when it is cut loose.

Work area

Roofing jack below work area

Roofing jack at roof edge

3 Attach a pair of roofing jacks just above the roof edge, and attach another pair just below the work area. Lay 2"- thick planks across each pair of jacks.

4 Measure between the nails to make sure the rough opening dimensions are accurate. Snap chalk lines on the shingles between the nails to mark the rough opening. Drive nails back through roof.

5 Use casing nails to attach a straight 1 × 4 flush along the inside edge of one cutting line. Use a nail set to drive the heads below the wood surface so they do not scratch the saw foot.

6 Cut through the shingles and sheathing along the marked line, using a circular saw and remodeler's blade set to maximum depth. (Use an old saw blade, because mineral particles in shingles will ruin a new blade.) Rest the saw foot on the 1 × 4 to protect it from scratches, and use the edge of the board as a guide. Reposition the 1 × 4 and cut along the remaining lines. **Do not stand or lean on the cutout area.**

7 After the cut section drops down onto the diagonal 2 × 4 brace, carefully lift it out of the hole. Remove the diagonal brace and continue with the skylight installation (pages 104 to 113). When the job is done, remove the roofing jacks, and fill the nail holes with roofing cement.

Temporary top plate

Sole plate: found only in platform framing

Temporary sole plate

Hydraulic jacks

Temporary supports for a platform-framed house must support the ceiling joists, since the ceiling platform carries the load of the upstairs structure. Platform framing can be identified by the sole plate to which the wall studs are nailed.

Braces

Whaler

Planned rough opening

Temporary supports for a balloon-framed house support the wall studs, which carry the upstairs load. The temporary support header, called a whaler, is anchored to the wall studs above the planned rough opening, and is supported by wall studs and bracing adjacent to the rough opening. Balloon framing can be identified by long wall studs that pass uncut through the floor to a sill plate resting on the foundation.

Making Temporary Supports

If your project requires you to remove more than one stud in a load-bearing wall, temporary supports will be needed while you do the framing. To identify a load-bearing wall, see page 13. The techniques for making temporary supports vary, depending on whether your house uses platform framing or balloon framing (see photos, left; and pages 10 to 11).

Platform framing is found in most homes built after 1930. To make temporary supports, use hydraulic jacks (page opposite) or a temporary stud wall (page 54). The stud wall method is the better choice if the supports must remain in place for more than one day.

If the ceiling and floor joists run parallel to the wall you are working on, use the method shown at the bottom of page 54.

Balloon framing is found in many homes built before 1930. To make temporary supports for balloon framing, use the method shown on page 55.

Some remodeling jobs require two temporary supports. For example, when making a large opening in an interior load-bearing wall, you must install supports on both sides of the wall (page 58).

Everything You Need:

Tools: tape measure, circular saw, hammer, ratchet, drill and spade bit, hydraulic jacks.

Materials: 2 x 4 lumber, 3" lag screws, 2" utility screws, 10d nails, cloths.

How to Support Platform Framing with Hydraulic Jacks when Joists Are Perpendicular to Wall

1 Measure width of planned rough opening, and add 4 ft. so temporary support will reach well past rough opening. Cut three 2 × 4s to that length. Nail two of the 2 × 4s together with 10d nails to make a top plate for temporary support. The remaining 2 × 4 will be the sole plate for the temporary support. Place the temporary sole plate on the floor 3 ft. from the wall, centering it on the planned rough opening.

2 Set hydraulic jacks on the temporary sole plate, 2 ft. in from the ends. (Use three jacks if opening will be more than 8 ft. wide.) For each jack, build a post by nailing together a pair of 2 × 4s. Posts should be about 4" shorter than the distance between the ceiling and the top of the jacks. Attach the posts to the top plate, 2 ft. from the ends, using countersunk lag screws.

Direction of joists

3 Cover the top of the plate with a thick layer of cloth to protect the ceiling from cracking, then lift the support structure onto the hydraulic jacks.

4 Adjust the support structure so the posts are exactly plumb, then raise the hydraulic jacks until the top plate just begins to lift the ceiling. Do not lift too far, or you may damage the floor and ceiling.

Alternate: How to Support Platform Framing with a Temporary Stud Wall (Joists Perpendicular to Wall)

1 Build a 2 × 4 stud wall that is 4 ft. wider than the planned wall opening and 1³/₄" shorter than the distance from floor to ceiling.

2 Raise the stud wall up and position it 3 ft. from the wall, centered on the planned rough opening.

3 Slide a 2 × 4 top plate between temporary wall and ceiling. Check to make sure wall is plumb, then drive shims under the top plate at 12" intervals until the wall is wedged tightly in place.

How to Support Platform Framing when Joists Are Parallel to Wall

1 Follow directions on page 53, except: Build two 4-ft.-long cross braces, using pairs of 2 × 4s nailed together. Attach the cross braces to the double top plate, 1 ft. from the ends, using counter-sunk lag screws.

2 Place a 2 × 4 sole plate directly over a floor joist, then set hydraulic jacks on the sole plate. For each jack, build a post 8" shorter than the jack-to-ceiling distance. Nail posts to top plate, 2 ft. from ends. Cover braces with cloth, and set support structure on jacks.

3 Adjust the support structure so the posts are exactly plumb, then pump the hydraulic jacks until the cross braces just begin to lift the ceiling. Do not lift too far, or you may damage the floor or ceiling.

How to Support Balloon Framing

1 Remove the wall surfaces around the rough opening from floor to ceiling (pages 38 to 41). Make a temporary support header (called a whaler) by cutting a 2 × 8 long enough to extend at least 20" past each side of the planned rough opening. Center the whaler against the wall studs, flush with the ceiling. Tack the whaler in place with 2" utility screws.

2 Cut two lengths of 2 × 4 to fit snugly between the bottom of the whaler and the floor. Slide 2 × 4s into place at the ends of the whaler, then attach them with nailing plates and 10d nails.

3 Drill two 3/16" holes through the whaler and into each stud it spans. Secure the whaler with 3/8" × 4" lag screws.

4 Drive shims between the bottom of each 2 × 4 and the floor to help secure the support structure.

After

Header made
from two
pieces of
MicroLam®

Post

Post

Spacing
blocks

Spacing
blocks

Nailing strip

Before

Load-bearing wall

When removing a wall, first tear off the wall surface, exposing the framing members. Do not cut
wall studs until you know if you are working with a
load-bearing wall, or a non-load-bearing (partition)
wall (page 13). If the wall is load-bearing, you will
need to install temporary supports (pages 52 to 55)
while cutting out the studs. When removing a load-
bearing wall, you must replace it with a permanent
header and posts strong enough to carry the structural weight once borne by the wall. The posts will
be hidden inside the adjacent walls after the wallboard is patched. The header will be visible, but
covering it with wallboard will help it blend in with
the ceiling. NOTE: Load-bearing walls more than 12 ft.
long should be removed only by a professional.

Removing & Building Walls

Removing an existing wall or building a new wall are easy ways to create more usable space without the expense of building an addition. By removing a wall, you can turn two small rooms into a large space perfect for family living. By adding new walls in a larger area, you can create a private space to use as a quiet study or as a new bedroom for a growing family.

The techniques for removing a wall vary greatly, depending on the location and structural function of the wall (see pages 11 to 13). Partition walls are relatively easy to work with, while load-bearing walls require special planning.

In addition to defining living areas and supporting the house structure, walls also hold the essential mechanical systems that run through your home. You will need to consider how your project affects electrical wiring, plumbing pipes, gas pipes, and heating and air-conditioning ductwork. Unless you are confident of your own skills, it is a good idea to have a professional make changes to these systems.

Included in this section:

- Removing a wall (pages 58 to 59)
- Installing a permanent header (pages 60 to 61)
- Building a partition wall (pages 62 to 65)

Materials for Building a Header

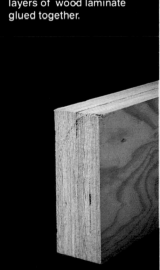

Beam made from 2 × 12s and plywood: 8-ft. maximum recommended span

Double 9¹⁄₂" MicroLam® beam: 10-ft. maximum recommended span. MicroLam framing members are made from thin layers of wood laminate glued together.

Double 11³⁄₈" MicroLam® beam: 11-ft maximum recommended span

12" GlueLam® beam: 12-ft. maximum recommended span. GlueLam beams are made from layers of dimension lumber laminated together. GlueLam beans can be stained and left exposed for an attractive appearance.

Manufactured support members are stronger and more durable than 2" dimension lumber, so they work well for building a header to replace a load-bearing wall. *Always consult your building inspector or a professional builder* when choosing materials and sizes for a support header.

Removing a Wall

When removing a wall, you must determine if you are working with a load-bearing wall, or a non-load-bearing (partition) wall. (See page 13.) When removing a load-bearing wall, you will need to make temporary supports and install a header.

To maintain some separation between joined rooms, you may choose to remove just a section of the wall.

Everything You Need:

Tools: tape measure, pencil, drill and bits, reciprocating saw, pry bar, hammer.

Materials (for installing a header): 2" dimension lumber, MicroLam® framing members, 10d nails.

How to Remove a Wall

1 Prepare the project site, remove the surfaces from the wall being removed, then remove or reroute any wiring, plumbing lines, or ductwork. (See pages 34 to 41.)

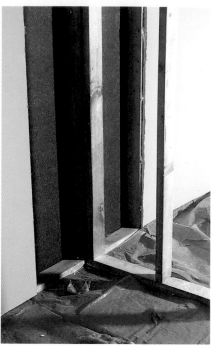

2 Remove the surface of the adjoining walls to expose the permanent studs.

3 Determine if the wall being removed is load-bearing or non-load-bearing (page 13). If the wall is load-bearing, install temporary supports on each side of the wall being removed (pages 52 to 55).

4 Remove studs by cutting them through the middle and prying them away from the sole plate and top plate.

Nailing stud

5 Remove the end stud on each end of the wall. If wall being removed is load-bearing, also remove any nailing studs or blocking in the adjoining walls directly behind the removed wall.

6 Make two cuts through the top plate, at least 3" apart, using a reciprocating saw or handsaw. Remove the cut section with a pry bar.

7 Remove the remaining sections of the top plate, using a pry bar.

8 Remove a 3"-wide section of sole plate, using a reciprocating saw. Pry out entire sole plate, using a pry bar. If removed wall was load-bearing, install a permanent header (page 60).

Tips for Removing a Section of Wall

When removing wall surfaces, expose the wall back to the first permanent studs at each side of the opening.

Leave a small portion of exposed sole plate to serve as the base for posts. In a load-bearing wall (A), leave 3" of sole plate to hold the double 2 × 4 post that will support the permanent header. In a non-load-bearing wall (B), leave 1 1/2" of exposed sole plate to hold one extra wall stud. Top plates should be removed over the entire width of the opening.

How to Install a Permanent Header when Removing a Load-bearing Wall

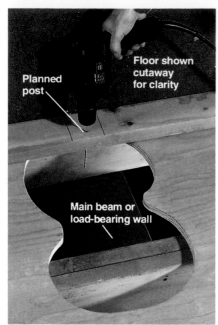

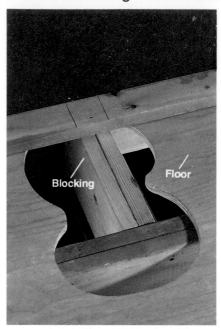

1 Mark the location of the planned support posts on the sole plate. Drill through the sole plate where support posts will rest to make sure there is a joist directly underneath. If not, install blocking under the post locations (step 2).

2 If necessary, cut and install double 2" blocking between joists. (You may need to cut into a finished ceiling to gain access to this space.) Blocking should be same size lumber as joists. Attach blocks to joists with 10d nails.

3 Build a support header to span the width of the removed wall, including the width of the support posts. See page 57 for header recommendations: in this project, the header is built with two lengths of MicroLam® joined with 10d nails.

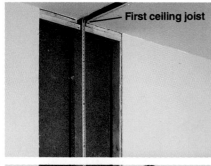

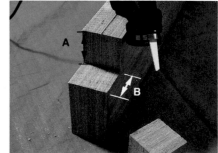

4 Lay the ends of the header on the sole plates. Find the length for each support post by measuring between the top of the header and the bottom of the first ceiling joist in from the wall.

5 Make support posts by cutting pairs of 2 × 4s to length and joining them side by side with wood glue and 10d nails.

6 Measure the thickness (A) and width (B) of the top plate at each end, then notch the top corners of the header to fit around the top plates, using a reciprocating saw.

7 Lift the header against the ceiling joists, then set the posts under the ends of the header. If the header will not fit due to sagging ceiling joists, then raise the joists by jacking up or shimming the temporary supports.

8 Toenail the posts to the header with 10d nails.

9 Check each post for plumb with a carpenter's level, and adjust it if necessary by tapping the bottom with a hammer. When post is plumb, mark a reference line on the sole plate, and toenail the bottom of each post to the sole plate.

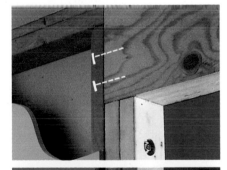

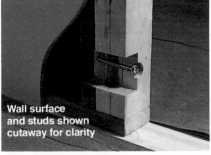

10 Cut 2 × 4 nailing strips and attach them to each side of the post and header with 10d nails. Nailing strips provide a surface for attaching new wallboard.

11 Cut and toenail spacing blocks to fit into the gaps between the permanent studs and the nailing strips. Patch and finish the wall and beam as directed on pages 118 to 121.

When removing a section of a wall, attach the posts to the wall studs with countersunk lag screws (bottom). Endnail the wall studs to the header with 10d nails (top).

Wall surface and studs shown cutaway for clarity

Building a Partition Wall

Partition walls divide spaces into rooms, but do not carry any significant structural weight. Because partition walls are not load-bearing, the framing techniques are simple. However, take care to make sure the new wall you build is plumb, straight, and perpendicular to the adjoining walls.

Interior partition walls usually are built with 2 × 4 lumber, but in some situations it is better to frame with 2 × 6 lumber (photo, left). Before finishing the walls with wallboard (pages 118 to 121), have the building inspector review your work. The inspector also may check to see that any required plumbing and wiring changes are complete.

Use 2 × 6 lumber to frame a new wall that must hold large plumbing pipes. Where wall plates must be cut to fit pipes, use metal straps to join the framing members (inset). For improved soundproofing, you can also fill walls with fiberglass insulation.

Everything You Need:

Tools: drill and twist bit, chalk line, tape measure, combination square, pencil, framing square, ladder, plumb bob, hammer.

Materials: framing lumber, 10d nails.

Variations for Fastening New Walls to Joists

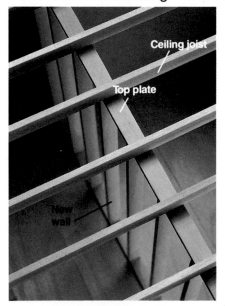

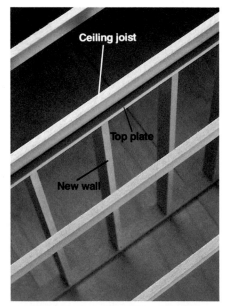

New wall perpendicular to joists: Attach the top plate and sole plate directly to the ceiling and floor joists with 10d nails.

New wall parallel to joists, but not aligned: Install 2 × 4 blocking between the joists every 2 ft., using 10d nails. Bottom of blocking should be flush with the edges of joists. Anchor plates with 10d nails driven into the blocking.

New wall aligned with parallel joists: Attach top plate to ceiling joist and sole plate to the floor, using 10d nails.

How to Build a Partition Wall

1 Mark the location of the new wall on the ceiling, then snap two chalk lines to outline the position of the new top plate. Locate the first ceiling joist or cross block by drilling into the ceiling between the lines, then measure to find the remaining joists.

2 Make the top and bottom wall plates by cutting two 2 × 4s to wall length. Lay the plates side by side, and use a combination square to outline the stud locations at 16" intervals.

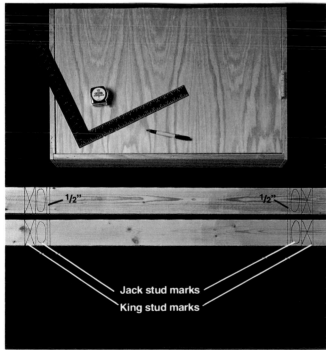

Jack stud marks
King stud marks

3 Mark the position of the door framing members on the top plate and sole plate, using Xs for king studs and Os for jack studs. The rough opening measured between the insides of jack studs should be about 1" wider than the actual width of the door to allow for adjustments during installation.

4 Position the top plate against the ceiling between the chalk lines, and use two 10d nails to tack it in place with the stud marks facing down. Use a framing square to make sure the plate is perpendicular to the adjoining walls, then anchor the plate to the joists with 10d nails.

(continued next page)

5 Determine position of sole plate by hanging a plumb bob from edge of the top plate near an adjoining wall so the plumb bob tip nearly touches the floor. When the plumb bob is motionless, mark its position on the floor. Repeat at the opposite end of top plate, then snap a chalk line between the marks to show the location of the sole plate edge.

6 Cut away the portion of the sole plate where the door framing will fit, then position the remaining pieces against the sole plate outline on the floor. On wood floors, anchor the sole plate pieces with 10d nails driven into the floor joists.

On concrete floors, attach the sole plate with a stud driver, available at rental centers. A stud driver fires a small gunpowder charge to drive a masonry nail through the framing member and into the concrete. Wear hearing protectors when using a stud driver.

7 Find the length of the first stud by measuring the distance between the sole plate and the top plate at the first stud mark. Add 1/8" to ensure a snug fit, and cut the stud to length.

8 Position the stud between the top plate and sole plate so the stud markings are covered.

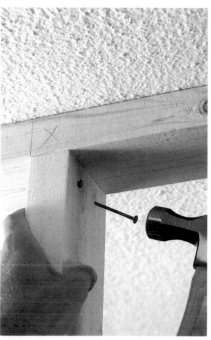

9 Attach the stud by toenailing through the sides of the studs and into the top plate and sole plate. Measure, cut, and install all remaining studs one at a time.

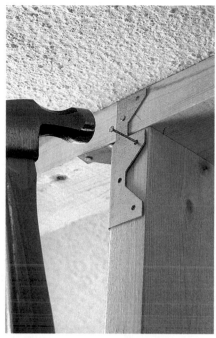

Option: Attach the studs to sole plate and top plate with metal connectors and 4d nails.

10 Frame the rough opening for the door (see pages 66 to 67).

11 Install 2 × 4 blocking between studs, 4 ft. from the floor. Arrange to have the wiring and any other utility work completed, then have your project inspected. Install wallboard and trim the wall as shown on pages 118 to 123.

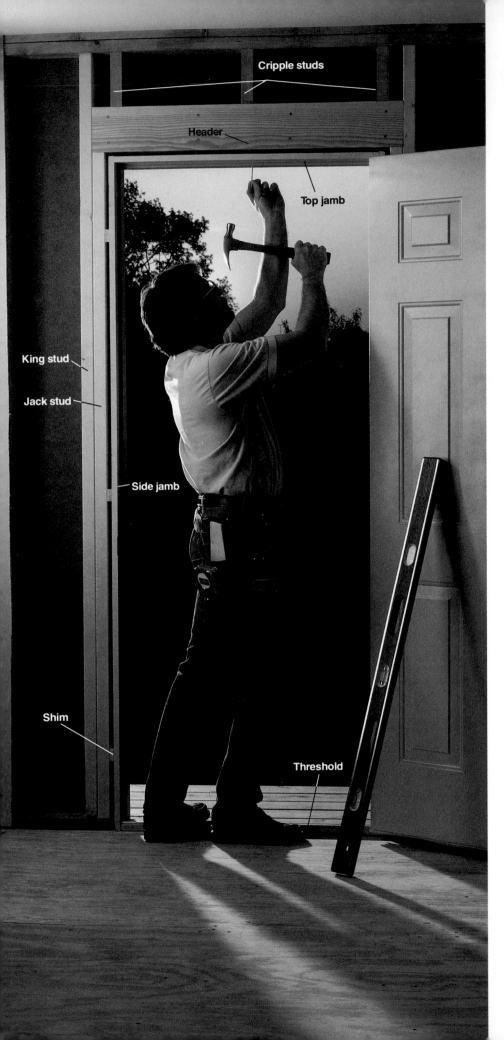

Cripple studs

Header

Top jamb

King stud

Jack stud

Side jamb

Shim

Threshold

Framing & Installing Doors

Your local home center carries many interior and exterior doors in stock sizes. For custom sizes, have the home center special-order the doors from the manufacturer. Special orders generally take three or four weeks for delivery.

For easy installation, buy "prehung" interior and exterior doors, which are already mounted in their jambs. Although unmounted doors are widely available, installing them is a complicated job that is best left to a professional.

When replacing an existing door, choosing a new unit the same size as the old door makes your work easier, because you can use framing members already in place.

This section shows:

- Framing a door opening (pages 67 to 71)

- Installing an interior door (pages 72 to 73)

- Installing an entry door (pages 74 to 77)

- Installing a storm door (pages 78 to 79)

- Installing a patio door (pages 80 to 84)

The following pages show installation techniques for wood-frame houses with lap siding. If your home exterior is stucco or masonry, see pages 46 to 49 for more information on working with these materials.

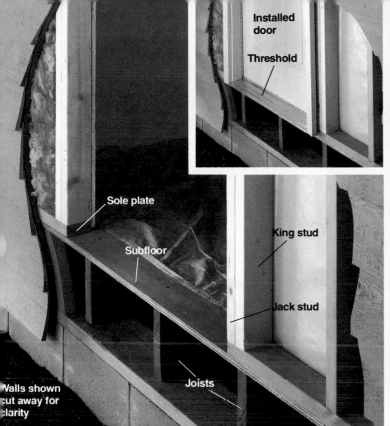

New door opening in a platform-framed house has studs that rest on a sole plate running across the top of the subfloor. The sole plate between the jack studs is cut away so the threshold for the new door can rest directly on the subfloor.

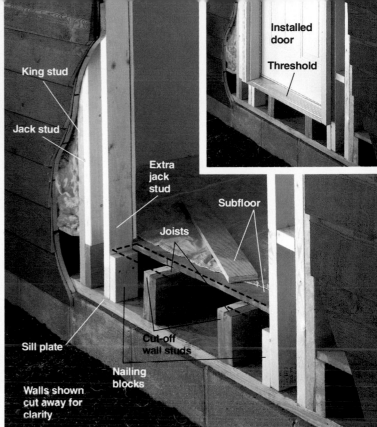

New door opening in a balloon-framed house has studs extending past the subfloor to rest on the sill plate. Jack studs rest either on the sill plate or on top of the joists. To provide a surface for the door threshold, install nailing blocks, and extend the subfloor out to the ends of the joists, using plywood.

Framing & Installing Doors
Framing a Door Opening

The rough opening for a new door should be framed after the interior preparation work is done (pages 34 to 49), but before the exterior wall surfaces are removed. The methods for framing the opening will vary, depending on whether your house is built with platform framing or balloon framing. (See photos, above; and pages 10 to 11.)

Always build temporary supports to hold up the ceiling if your project requires that you cut or remove more than one stud in a load-bearing wall (pages 52 to 55).

Everything You Need:

Tools: tape measure, pencil, level, plumb bob, reciprocating saw, circular saw, handsaw, hammer, pry bar, nippers.

Materials: 2" dimension lumber, 3/8" plywood, 10d nails.

When framing a door opening in a new wall, install the door framing members at the same time you install the wall studs (pages 62 to 65). Cut and install cripple studs to reach between the top of the header and the top plate. Cripples should be spaced at the same interval as the wall studs, and anchored with 10d nails.

How to Frame a Door Opening

1 Prepare the project site and remove the interior wall surfaces (pages 35 to 41).

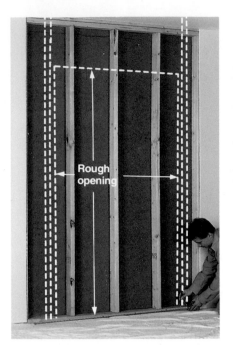

2 Measure and mark the rough opening width on the sole plate. Mark the locations of the jack studs and king studs on the sole plate. (Where practical, use existing studs as king studs.)

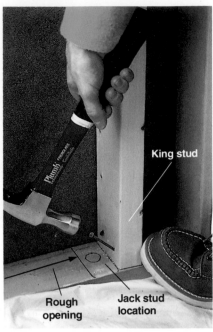

3 Measure and cut king studs to fit between the sole plate and top plate. Position the king studs and toenail them to the sole plate with 10d nails.

4 Check the king studs with a level to make sure they are plumb, then toenail them to the top plate with 10d nails.

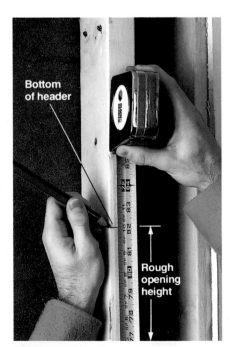

5 Measuring from the floor, mark the rough opening height on one king stud. For most doors, the recommended rough opening is 1/2" greater than the height of the door jamb. This line marks the bottom of the door header.

6 Measure and mark where the top of the header will fit against a king stud. Header size depends on the distance between the king studs (page 14). Use a level to extend the lines across the intermediate studs to the opposite king stud.

68

Cripple stud

Top of header

7 Cut two jack studs to reach from the top of the sole plate to the rough opening marks on the king studs. Nail the jack studs to the king studs with 10d nails driven every 12". **Make temporary supports** (pages 52 to 55) if wall is load-bearing and you are removing more than one stud.

8 Use a circular saw set to maximum blade depth to cut through the old studs that will be removed. The remaining stud sections will be used as cripple studs for the door frame. Do not cut king studs. Make additional cuts 3" below the first cuts, then finish the cuts with a handsaw.

9 Knock out the 3" stud sections, then tear out the rest of the studs with a pry bar. Clip away any exposed nails, using a nippers.

10 Build a header to fit between the king studs on top of the jack studs. Use two pieces of 2" dimension lumber sandwiched around 3/8" plywood (page 88). Attach the header to the jack studs, king studs, and cripple studs, using 10d nails.

11 Use a reciprocating saw to cut through the sole plate next to each jack stud, then remove the sole plate with a pry bar. Cut off any exposed nails or anchors, using a nippers.

How to Frame a Door Opening in a Balloon-framed House

1 Prepare the project site and remove the interior wall surfaces (pages 35 to 41). Select two existing studs to use as king studs. The distance between selected studs must be at least 3" wider than the planned rough opening. Measuring from the floor, mark the rough opening height on a king stud.

2 Measure and mark where the top of the header will fit against the king stud. Header size depends on the distance between the king studs (page 14). Use a level to extend the line across the studs to the opposite king stud.

3 Use a reciprocating saw to cut open the subfloor between the studs, then remove any fire blocking in the stud cavities. This allows access to the sill plate when installing the jack studs. If you will be removing more than one wall stud, **make temporary supports** (pages 52 to 55).

4 Use a circular saw to cut studs along the lines marking the top of header. Do not cut king studs. Make two additional cuts on each cut stud, 3" below the first cut and 6" above the floor. Finish cuts with a handsaw, then knock out 3" sections with a hammer. Remove the studs with a pry bar (page 69).

5 Cut two jack studs to reach from the top of the sill plate to the rough opening mark on the king studs. Nail the jack studs to the king studs with 10d nails driven every 12".

6 Build a header to fit between the king studs on top of the jack studs, using two pieces of 2" dimension lumber sandwiched around 3/8" plywood (page 88). Attach the header to the jack studs, king studs, and cripple studs, using 10d nails.

7 Measure and mark the rough opening width on the header. Use a plumb bob to mark the rough opening on the sill plate (inset).

8 Cut and install additional jack studs, as necessary, to frame the sides of the rough opening. Toenail the jack studs to the top plate and the sill plate, using 10d nails. NOTE: You may have to go to the basement to do this.

9 Install horizontal 2 × 4 blocking, where necessary, between the studs on each side of the rough opening, using 10d nails. Blocking should be installed at the lockset location and at the hinge locations on the new door.

10 Remove the exterior wall surface as directed on pages 44 to 49.

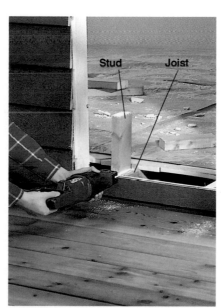

11 Cut off the ends of the exposed studs flush with the tops of the floor joists, using a reciprocating saw or handsaw.

12 Install 2 × 4 nailing blocks next to the jack studs and joists, flush with the tops of the floor joists (See NOTE in Step 8). Reinstall any fire-blocking that was removed. Patch the subfloor area between the jack studs with plywood to form a flat, level surface for the door threshold.

Top jamb

Side jamb

Case molding

Installing an Interior Door

Install prehung interior doors after the framing work is completed and the wallboard has been installed (see pages 118 to 121). If the rough opening for the door has been framed accurately, installing the door takes about an hour.

Most standard prehung doors are sized to fit walls with 2 x 4 construction. If you have thicker walls, you can special-order a door to match, or you can add jamb extensions to a standard-size door (photo, below).

Everything You Need:

Tools: level, hammer, handsaw.

Materials: wood shims, 8d casing nails.

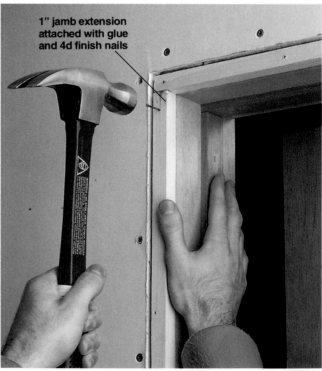

1" jamb extension attached with glue and 4d finish nails

Standard prehung doors have 4 9/16"-wide jambs, and are designed for 2 x 4 wall construction with 1/2" wallboard. If your walls are thicker, you will need to attach jamb extensions to the edge of the door frame. For example, if your walls are built with 2 x 6 studs, extend the jambs by attaching 3/4"-wide wood strips to the jamb edges.

How to Install a Prehung Interior Door

1 Slide the door unit into the framed opening so the edges of the jambs are flush with the wall surface and the hinge side jamb is plumb.

2 Insert pairs of wood shims driven from opposite directions into the space between the framing members and the hinge side jamb, spaced every 12". Check the hinge-side jamb to make sure it is still plumb and does not bow.

3 Anchor the hinge-side jamb with 8d casing nails driven through the jamb and shims and into the jack stud.

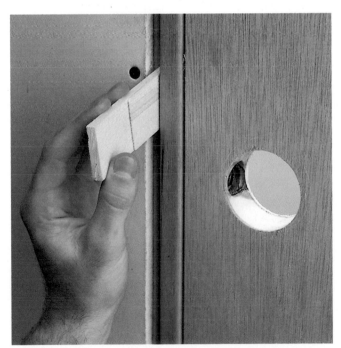

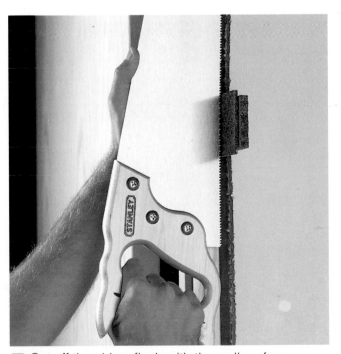

4 Insert pairs of shims in the space between the framing members and the latch-side jamb and top jamb, spaced every 12". With the door closed, adjust the shims so the gap between door edge and jamb is 1/8" wide. Drive casing nails through the jambs and shims and into the framing members.

5 Cut off the shims flush with the wall surface, using a handsaw. Hold the saw vertically to prevent damage to the door jamb or wall. Finish the door and install the lockset as directed by the manufacturer. See pages 118 to 123 to finish the walls and trim the door.

Installing an Entry Door

Prehung entry doors come in many styles, but all are installed using the same basic methods. Because entry doors are very heavy—some large units weigh several hundred pounds—make sure you have help before beginning installation.

To speed your work, do the indoor surface removal and framing work in advance. Before installing the door, make sure you have purchased all necessary locksets and hardware. After installation, protect your door against the weather by painting or staining it immediately, and by adding a storm door (pages 78 to 79) as soon as possible.

Everything You Need:

Tools: metal snips, hammer, level, pencil, circular saw, wood chisel, nail set, caulk gun.

Materials: building paper, drip edge, wood shims, fiberglass insulation, 10d casing nails, silicone caulk.

How to Install an Entry Door

Brick molding

1 Remove the door unit from its packing. Do not remove the retaining brackets that hold the door closed. Remove the exterior surface material inside the framed opening as directed on pages 44 to 49.

2 Test-fit the door unit, centering it in the rough opening. Check to make sure door is plumb. If necessary, shim under the lower side jamb until the door is plumb and level.

3 Trace outline of brick molding on siding. NOTE: If you have vinyl or metal siding, enlarge the outline to make room for the extra trim moldings required by these sidings. Remove the door unit after finishing the outline.

4 Cut the siding along the outline, just down to the sheathing, using a circular saw. Stop just short of the corners to prevent damage to the siding that will remain.

5 Finish the cuts at the corners with a sharp wood chisel.

6 Cut 8"-wide strips of building paper and slide them between the siding and sheathing at the top and sides of the opening, to shield framing members from moisture. Bend paper around the framing members and staple it in place.

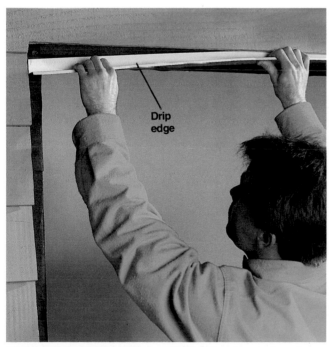

Drip edge

7 To provide an added moisture barrier, cut a piece of drip edge to fit the width of the rough opening, then slide between the siding and the building paper at the top of the opening. Do not nail the drip edge.

8 Apply several thick beads of silicone caulk to the subfloor at the bottom of the door opening. Also apply silicone caulk over the building paper on the front edges of the jack studs and header.

(continued next page)

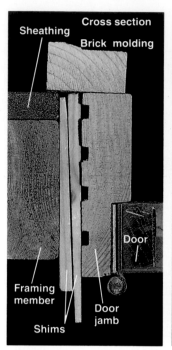

9 Center the door unit in the rough opening, and push the brick molding tight against the sheathing. Have a helper hold the door unit in place until it is nailed in place.

10 From inside, place pairs of hardwood wedge shims together to form flat shims (inset), and insert shims into the gaps between the door jambs and framing members. Insert shims at the lockset and hinge locations, and every 12" thereafter.

Cross section

Sheathing

Brick molding

Door

Framing member

Shims

Door jamb

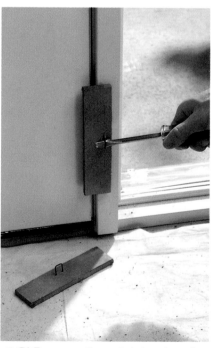

11 Make sure the door unit is plumb. Adjust the shims, if necessary, until the door is plumb and level. Fill the gaps between the jambs and the framing members with loosely packed fiberglass insulation.

12 From outside, drive 10d casing nails through the door jambs and into the framing members at each shim location. Use a nail set to drive the nail heads below the surface of the wood.

13 Remove the retaining brackets installed by the manufacturer, then open and close the door to make sure it works properly.

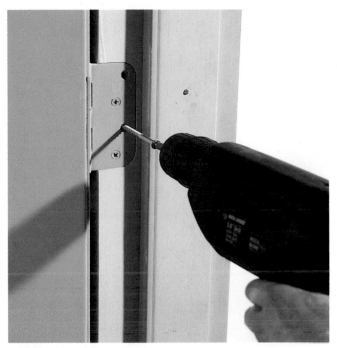

14 Remove two of the screws on the top hinge and replace them with long anchor screws (usually included with the unit). These anchor screws will penetrate into the framing members to strengthen the installation.

15 Anchor brick molding to the framing members with 10d galvanized casing nails driven every 12". Use a nail set to drive the nail heads below the surface of the wood.

16 Adjust the door threshold to create a tight seal, following manufacturer's recommendations.

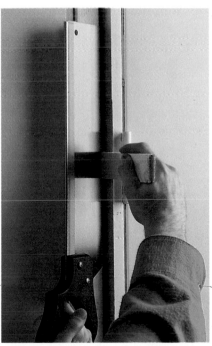

17 Cut off the shims flush with the framing members, using a handsaw.

18 Apply silicone caulk around the entire door unit. Fill nail holes with caulk. Finish the door and install the lockset as directed by the manufacturer. See pages 118 to 123 to finish the walls and trim the interior of the door.

Installing a Storm Door

Install a storm door to improve the appearance and weather-resistance of an old entry door, or to protect a newly installed door against weathering. In all climates, adding a storm door can extend the life of an entry door by years.

When buying a storm door, look for models that have a solid inner core and seamless outer shell construction. Carefully note the dimensions of your door opening, measuring from the inside edges of the entry door's brick molding. Choose a storm door that opens from the same side as your entry door.

Everything You Need:

Tools: tape measure, pencil, plumb bob, hacksaw, hammer, drill and bits, screwdrivers.

Materials: storm door unit, wood spacer strips, 4d casing nails.

Adjustable sweeps help make storm doors weathertight. Before installing the door, attach the sweep to the bottom of the door. After the door is mounted, adjust the height of the sweep so it brushes the top of the sill lightly when the door is closed.

How To Cut a Storm Door Frame to Fit a Door Opening

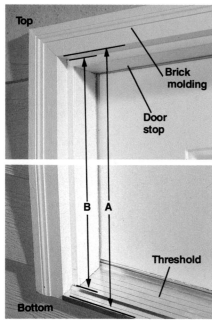

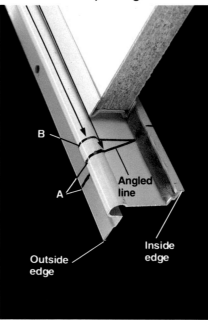

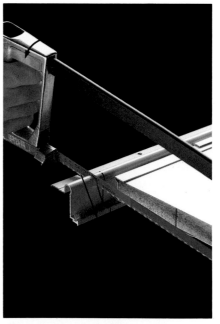

1 Because entry door thresholds are slanted, the bottom of the storm door frame needs to be cut to match the threshold angle. First, measure from the threshold to the top of the door opening along the corner of the brick molding (A), and along the front edge of entry door stop (B).

2 Subtract 1/8" from measurements A and B to allow for small adjustments when the door is installed. Measuring from the top of the storm door frame, mark adjusted points A and B on the corner bead. Draw a line from point A to outside edge of frame and from point B to inside edge. Draw an angled line from point A on corner bead to point B on the inside edge.

3 Use a hacksaw to cut down through the bottom of the storm door frame, following the angled line. Make sure to hold the hacksaw at the same slant as the angled line to ensure that the the cut will be smooth and straight.

How to Fit & Install a Storm Door

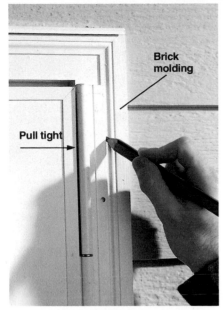

1 Position the storm door in the opening and pull the frame tight against the brick molding on the hinge side of the storm door, then draw a reference line onto the brick molding, following the edge of the storm door frame.

2 Push the storm door tight against the brick molding on the latch side, then measure the gap between the reference line and the hinge side of the door frame. If the distance is greater than 3/8", then spacer strips must be installed to ensure the door will fit snugly.

3 To install spacers, remove the door then nail thin strips of wood to the inside of the brick molding at storm door hinge locations. The thickness of the wood strips should be 1/8" less than the gap measured in step 5.

4 Replace the storm door and push it tightly against the brick molding on the hinge side. Drill pilot holes through the hinge side frame of the storm door and into the brick molding, then attach the frame with mounting screws spaced every 12".

5 Remove any spacer clips holding the frame to the storm door. With the storm door closed, drill pilot holes and attach the latch side frame to the brick molding. Use a coin to keep an even gap between the storm door and the storm door frame.

6 Center the top piece of the storm door frame on top of the frame sides. Drill pilot holes and screw the top piece to the brick molding. Adjust the bottom sweep, then attach locks and latch hardware as directed by the manufacturer.

Installing a Patio Door

For easy installation, buy a patio door with the door panels already mounted in preassembled frames. Avoid patio doors sold with frame kits that require complicated assembly.

Because patio doors have very long bottom sills and top jambs, they are susceptible to bowing and warping. To avoid these problems, be very careful to install the patio door so it is level and plumb, and to anchor the unit securely to framing members. Yearly caulking and touch-up painting helps prevent moisture from warping the jambs.

Everything You Need:

Tools: pencil, hammer, circular saw, wood chisel, stapler, caulk gun, pry bar, level, cordless screwdriver, handsaw, drill and bits.

Materials: shims, drip edge, building paper, silicone caulk, 10d casing nails, 3" wood screw, sill nosing.

Patio Door Accessory

Screen doors, if not included with the unit, can be ordered from most patio door manufacturers. Screen doors have spring-mounted rollers that fit into a narrow track on the outside of the patio door threshold.

Installation Tips

Heavy glass panels may be removed if you must install the door without help. Reinstall the panels after the frame has been placed in the rough opening and nailed at opposite corners. To remove and install the panels, remove the stop rail, found on the top jamb of the door unit.

Adjust the bottom rollers after installation is complete. Remove the coverplate on the adjusting screw, found on the inside edge of the bottom rail. Turn the screw in small increments until the door rolls smoothly along the track without binding when it is opened and closed.

Tips for Installing French-style Patio Doors

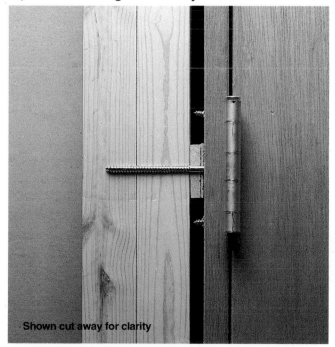

Shown cut away for clarity

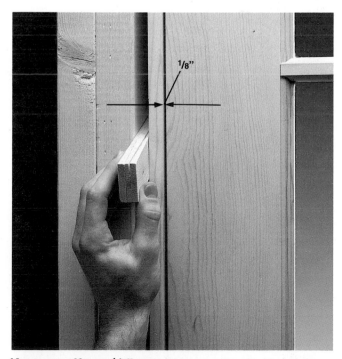

1/8"

Provide extra support for door hinges by replacing the center mounting screw on each hinge with a 3" wood screw. These long screws extend through the side jambs and deep into the framing members.

Keep a uniform 1/8" gap between the door and the side jambs and top jamb to ensure that the door will swing freely without binding. Check this gap frequently as you shim around the door unit.

How to Install a Patio Door

1 Prepare the work area and remove the interior wall surfaces (pages 35 to 41), then frame the rough opening for the patio door (pages 66 to 71). Remove the exterior surfaces inside the framed opening (pages 44 to 47).

2 Test-fit the door unit, centering it in the rough opening. Check to make sure door is plumb. If necessary, shim under the lower side jamb until the door is plumb and level. Have a helper hold the door in place while it is unattached.

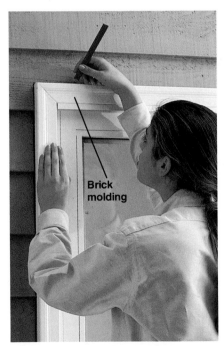

3 Trace the outline of the brick molding onto the siding, then remove the door unit. NOTE: If you have vinyl or metal siding, enlarge the outline to make room for the extra trim moldings required by these sidings.

4 Cut the siding along the outline, just down to the sheathing, using a circular saw. Stop just short of the corners to prevent damage to the siding that will remain. Finish the cuts at the corners with a sharp wood chisel.

5 To provide an added moisture barrier, cut a piece of drip edge to fit the width of the rough opening, then slide it between the siding and the existing building paper at the top of the opening. Do not nail the drip edge.

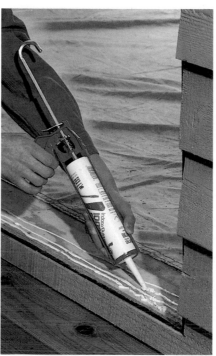

6 Cut 8"-wide strips of building paper and slide them between the siding and the sheathing. Bend the paper around the framing members and staple it in place.

7 Apply several thick beads of silicone caulk to the subfloor at the bottom of the door opening.

8 Apply silicone caulk around the front edge of the framing members, where the siding meets the building paper.

9 Center the patio door unit in the rough opening so the brick molding is tight against the sheathing. Have a helper hold the door unit from outside until it is shimmed and nailed in place.

10 Check the door threshold to make sure it is level. If necessary, shim under the lower side jamb until the patio door unit is level.

(continued next page)

11 If there are gaps between the threshold and subfloor, insert shims coated with caulk into the gaps, spaced every 6". Shims should be snug, but not so tight that they cause the threshold to bow. Clear off excess caulk immediately.

12 Place pairs of hardwood wedge shims together to form flat shims. Insert the shims into the gaps between the side jambs and the jack studs, spaced every 12". For sliding doors, shim behind the strike plate for the door latch.

13 Insert shims into the gap between the top jamb and the header, spaced every 12".

14 From outside, drive 10d casing nails, spaced every 12", through the brick molding and into the framing members. Use a nail set to drive the nail heads below the surface of the wood.

15 From inside, drive 10d casing nails through the door jambs and into the framing members at each shim location. Use a nail set to drive the nail heads below the surface of the wood.

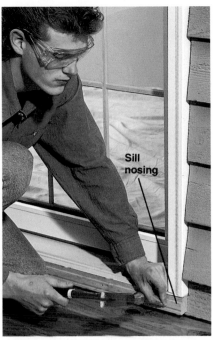

16 Remove one of the screws on the stop block found in the center of the threshold. Replace the screw with a 3" wood screw driven into the subfloor as an anchor.

17 Cut off the shims flush with the face of the framing members, using a handsaw. Fill gaps around the door jambs and beneath the threshold with loosely packed fiberglass insulation.

18 Reinforce and seal the edge of the threshold by installing sill nosing under the threshold and against the wall. Drill pilot holes and attach the sill nosing with 10d casing nails.

19 Make sure the drip edge is tight against the top brick molding, then apply silicone caulk along the top of the drip edge and along the outside edge of the side brick moldings. Fill all exterior nail holes with silicone caulk.

20 Caulk completely around the sill nosing, using your finger to press the caulk into cracks. As soon as the caulk is dry, paint the sill nosing. Finish the door and install the lockset as directed by the manufacturer. See pages 118 to 123 to finish the walls and trim the interior of the door.

Header

Angled stud

Jambs

Shims

Double rough sill

Insulation

Jack stud

Cripple studs

King stud

Framing & Installing Windows

Most good windows must be custom-ordered several weeks in advance. To save time, do the interior framing work before the window unit arrives. But never open the outside wall surface until you have the window and accessories, and are ready to install them.

Follow the manufacturer's specifications for rough opening size when framing for a window. The listed opening usually is 1" wider and 1/2" higher than the actual dimension of the window unit.

This section shows:
- Framing a window opening
  (pages 87 to 89)
- Installing a window
  (pages 90 to 93)
- Installing a bay window
  (pages 94 to 103)
- Framing & installing a skylight
  (pages 104 to 113)

The following pages show techniques for wood-frame houses with siding. If your home's exterior is stucco or masonry, see pages 46 to 49 for more information. If your house has balloon framing (page 11), use the method shown on page 70 (steps 1 to 6) to install a header.

If you have masonry walls, or if you are installing polymer-coated windows, you may want to attach your window using masonry clips instead of nails (page 93).

Everything You Need:

Tools: tape measure, pencil, combination square, hammer, level, circular saw, handsaw, pry bar, nippers, drill and bits, reciprocating saw, stapler, nail set, caulk gun.

Materials: 10d nails, 2" dimension lumber, 3/8" plywood, shims, building paper, drip edge, casing nails (16d, 8d), fiberglass insulation, silicone caulk.

How to Frame a Window Opening

1 Prepare the project site and re-move the interior wall surfaces (pages 35 to 41). Measure and mark rough opening width on sole plate. Mark the locations of the jack studs and king studs on sole plate. Where practical, use exist-ing studs as king studs.

2 Measure and cut king studs, as needed, to fit between the sole plate and top plate. Position the king studs and toenail them to the sole plate with 10d nails.

3 Check the king studs with a level to make sure they are plumb, then toenail them to the top plate with 10d nails.

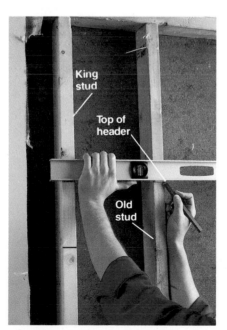

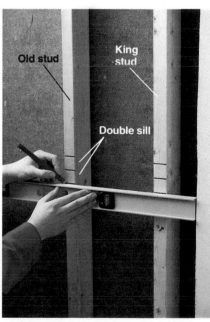

4 Measuring from the floor, mark the rough opening height on one of the king studs. For most windows, the recommended rough opening is 1/2" taller than the height of the window frame. This line marks the bottom of the window header.

5 Measure and mark where the top of the window header will fit against the king stud. The header size depends on the dis-tance between the king studs (page 14). Use a carpenter's level to extend the lines across the old studs to the opposite king stud.

6 Measure down from header line and outline the double rough sill on the king stud. Use a carpen-ter's level to extend the lines across the old studs to the opposite king stud. **Make temporary supports** (pages 52 to 55) if you will be removing more than one stud.

(continued next page)

7 Use a circular saw set to maximum blade depth to cut through the old studs along the lines marking the bottom of the rough sill, and along the lines marking the top of the header. Do not cut the king studs. On each stud, make an additional cut about 3" above the first cut. Finish the cuts with a handsaw.

8 Knock out the 3" stud sections, then tear out the old studs inside the rough opening, using a pry bar. Clip away any exposed nails, using a nippers. The remaining sections of the cut studs will serve as cripple studs for the window.

9 Build a header to fit between the king studs on top of the jack studs, using two pieces of 2" dimension lumber sandwiched around 3/8" plywood.

10 Cut two jack studs to reach from the top of the sole plate to the bottom header lines on the king studs. Nail the jack studs to the king studs with 10d nails driven every 12". NOTE: On a balloon-frame house the jack studs will reach to the sill plate, or only to the subfloor, if you are working on the second story (page 67).

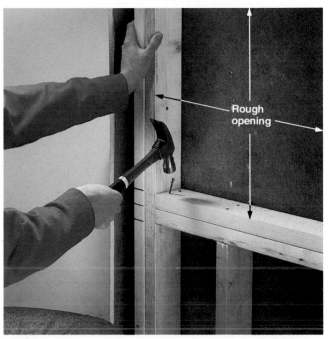

11 Position the header on the jack studs, using a hammer if necessary. Attach the header to the king studs, jack studs, and cripple studs, using 10d nails.

12 Build the rough sill to reach between the jack studs by nailing a pair of 2 × 4s together. Position the rough sill on the cripple studs, and nail it to the jack studs and cripple studs with 10d nails.

Variations for Round-top Windows

Create a template to help you mark the rough opening on the sheathing. Scribe the outline of the curved frame on cardboard, allowing an extra 1/2" for adjustments within the rough opening. A 1/4" × 1 1/4" metal washer makes a good spacer for scribing the outline. Cut out the template along the scribed line.

Tape the template to the sheathing, with the top flush against the header. Use the template as a guide for attaching diagonal framing members across the top corners of the framed opening. The diagonal members should just touch the template. Outline the template on the sheathing as a guide for cutting the rough opening (page 44).

How to Install a Window

1 Remove the exterior wall surface as directed on pages 44 to 49, then test-fit the window, centering it in the rough opening. Support the window with wood blocks and shims placed under the bottom jamb. Check to make sure the window is plumb and level, and adjust the shims, if necessary.

2 Trace the outline of the brick molding on the siding. NOTE: If you have vinyl or metal siding, enlarge the outline to make room for the extra J-channel moldings required by these sidings (page 115). Remove the window after finishing the outline.

3 Cut the siding along the outline just down to the sheathing. For a round-top window, use a reciprocating saw held at a shallow angle. For straight cuts, you can use a circular saw adjusted so blade depth equals the thickness of the siding, then use a sharp chisel to complete the cuts at the corners (page 75).

4 Cut 8"-wide strips of building paper and slide them between the siding and sheathing around the entire window opening. Bend the paper around the framing members and staple it in place.

5 Cut a length of drip edge to fit over the top of the window, then slide it between the siding and building paper. For round-top windows, use flexible vinyl drip edge; for rectangular windows, use rigid metal drip edge (inset).

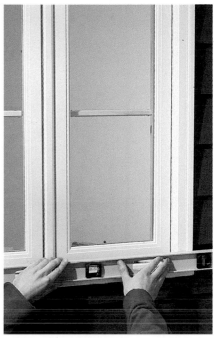

6 Insert the window in the opening, and push the brick molding tight against the sheathing.

7 Check to make sure the window is level.

8 If the window is perfectly level, nail both bottom corners of the brick molding with 10d casing nails. If window is not perfectly level, nail only at the higher of the two bottom corners.

9 If necessary, have a helper adjust the shim under the low corner of the window from the inside, until the window is level.

10 From outside, drive 10d casing nails through the brick molding and into the framing members near the remaining corners of the window.

(continued next page)

11 Place pairs of shims together to form flat shims. From inside, insert shims into the gaps between the jambs and framing members, spaced every 12". On round-top windows, also shim between the angled braces and curved jamb.

12 Adjust the shims so they are snug, but not so tight that they cause the jambs to bow. On multiple-unit windows, make sure the shims under the mull posts are tight.

13 Use a straightedge to check the side jambs to make sure they do not bow. Adjust the shims, if necessary, until the jambs are flat. Open and close the window to make sure it works properly.

14 At each shim location, drill a pilot hole, then drive an 8d casing nail through the jamb and shims and into the framing member, being careful not to damage the window. Drive the nail heads below the wood surface with a nail set.

15 Fill the gaps between the window jambs and the framing members with loosely packed fiberglass insulation. Wear work gloves when handling insulation.

Brick
molding

16 Trim the shims flush with the framing members, using a handsaw.

17 From outside, drive 10d galvanized casing nails, spaced every 12", through the brick moldings and into the framing members. Drive all nail heads below the wood surface with a nail set.

18 Apply silicone caulk around the entire window unit. Fill nail holes with caulk. See pages 118 to 123 to finish the walls and trim the interior of the window.

Installation Variation: Masonry Clips

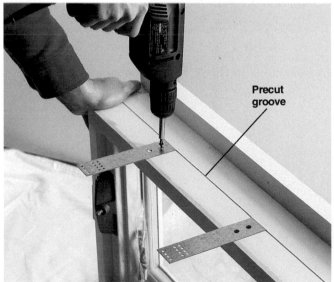

Precut
groove

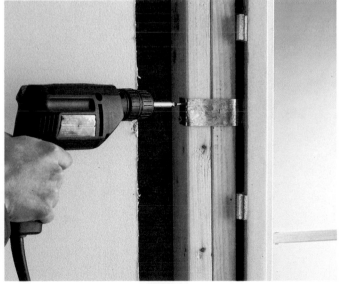

Use metal masonry clips when the brick molding on a window cannot be nailed because it rests against a masonry or brick surface. The masonry clips hook into precut grooves in the window jambs (above, left), and are attached to the jambs with utility screws. After the window unit is positioned in the rough opening, the masonry clips are bent around the framing members and anchored with

utility screws (above, right). NOTE: masonry clips also can be used in ordinary lap siding installations if you want to avoid making nail holes in the smooth surface of the brick moldings. For example, windows that are precoated with polymer-based paint can be installed with masonry clips so that the brick moldings are not punctured with nails.

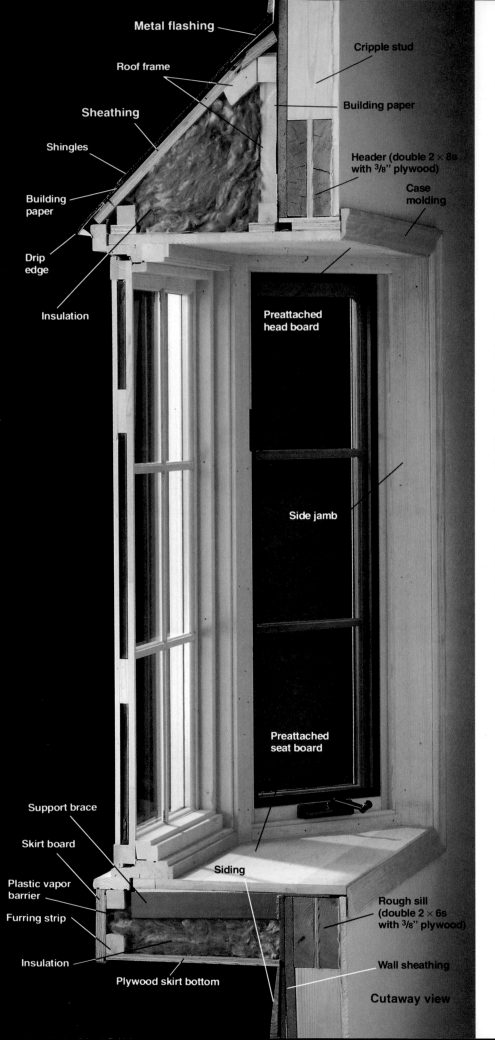

Metal flashing

Roof frame

Sheathing

Shingles

Building paper

Drip edge

Insulation

Cripple stud

Building paper

Header (double 2 × 8s with 3/8" plywood)

Case molding

Preattached head board

Side jamb

Preattached seat board

Support brace

Skirt board

Plastic vapor barrier

Furring strip

Insulation

Siding

Plywood skirt bottom

Rough sill (double 2 × 6s with 3/8" plywood)

Wall sheathing

Cutaway view

Installing a Bay Window

Modern bay windows are pre-assembled for easy installation, but you should still plan on several days to complete the work. Bay windows are large and heavy, and installing them requires special techniques. Have at least one helper to assist you, and try to schedule the work when the chance of rain is small. Use prebuilt bay window accessories (page opposite) to speed your work.

A large bay window can weigh several hundred pounds, so it must be anchored securely to framing members in the wall, and supported by braces attached to framing members below the window. Some window manufacturers include cable-support hardware that can be used instead of metal support braces.

Everything You Need:

Tools: circular saw, caulk gun, hammer, screw gun, framing square, tape measure, level, screwdriver, chisel, stapler, metal snips, roofing knife, T-bevel, utility knife.

Materials: bay window, prebuilt roof skirt, metal support brackets, galvanized utility screws (2", 2 1/2", 3"), building paper, sheet plastic, fiberglass insulation, 2 × 2 lumber, 5 1/2" skirt board, 3/4" exterior-grade plywood, shingles, roofing cement, wood shims, galvanized casing nails (16d, 8d), silicone caulk.

Prebuilt Accessories for Bay Windows

For easy installation, use prebuilt accessories when installing a bay window. Roof frames (A) come complete with sheathing (B), metal top flashing (C) and step flashing (D) and can be special-ordered at home centers that sell bay windows. You will need to specify the exact size of your window unit, and the angle (pitch) you want for the roof. You can cover the roof inexpensively with building paper and shingles, or order a copper or aluminum shell from your home center. Metal support braces (E) and skirt boards (F) can be ordered at your home center if they are not included with the window unit. Use two braces for bay windows up to 5 ft. wide, and three braces for larger windows. Skirt boards are clad with aluminum or vinyl, and can be cut to fit with a circular saw or power miter saw.

Framing a Bay Window

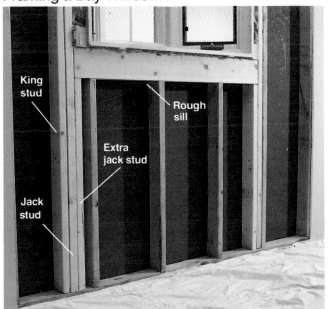

Bay window framing resembles that for a standard window, except that it requires an extra-strong rough sill built from a pair of 2 × 6s sandwiched around a layer of 3/8" plywood (page 88). Because the sill carries considerable weight, extra jack studs are installed under each end of the sill. See pages 86 to 89 for basic window framing techniques.

Roof Framing Variation

Build an enclosure above the bay window if the roof soffit overhangs the window. Build a 2 × 2 frame (top) to match the angles of the bay window, and attach the frame securely to the wall and overhanging soffit. Install a vapor barrier and insulation (page 99), then finish the enclosure so it matches the house siding (bottom).

How to Install a Bay Window

1 Prepare project site and remove interior wall surfaces (pages 35 to 41), then frame rough opening (pages 87 to 89). Remove exterior wall surface as directed on pages 44 to 49. Mark a section of siding directly below rough opening for removal. Width of marked area should equal that of window unit, and height should equal that of skirt board.

2 Set the blade on a circular saw just deep enough to cut through the siding, then cut along the outline. Stop just short of the corners to avoid damaging the siding outside the outline. Use a sharp chisel to complete the corner cuts (page 75). Remove the cut siding inside the outline.

3 Position the support braces along the rough sill within the widest part of the bay window and above the cripple stud locations. Add cripple studs to match support brace locations if necessary. Draw outlines of the braces on the top of the sill. Use a chisel or circular saw to notch the sill to a depth equal to the thickness of the support braces.

4 Slide the support braces down between the siding and the sheathing. You may need to pry the siding material away from the sheathing slightly to make room for the braces. NOTE: On stucco, you will need to chisel notches in masonry wall surface to fit the support braces.

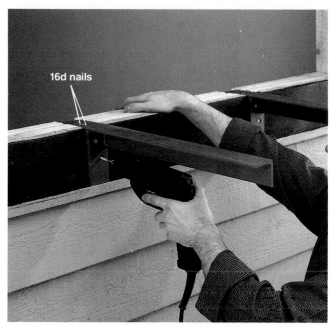

16d nails

5 Attach the braces to the rough sill with galvanized 16d nails. Drive 3" utility screws through the front of the braces and into the rough sill to prevent twisting.

6 Lift the bay window onto the support braces and slide it into the rough opening. Center the window in the opening.

7 Check the window unit to make sure it is level. If necessary, drive shims under the low side to level the window. Temporarily brace the outside bottom edge of the window with 2 × 4s to keep it from moving on the braces.

Sheathing

8 Set the roof frame on top of the window, with sheathing loosely tacked in place. Trace the outline of the window and roof unit onto the siding. Leave a gap of about 1/2" around the roof unit to allow room for the flashing and shingles.

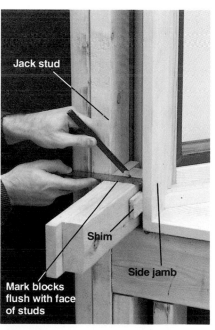

Jack stud

Shim

Side jamb

Mark blocks flush with face of studs

9 Mark and cut wood blocks to bridge the gap between side jambs and studs, if gap is more than 1" wide. (Smaller gaps require no blocks.) Leave a small space for inserting wood shims. Remove the window, then attach blocks every 12" along the studs.

(continued next page)

10 Cut the siding just down to the sheathing along the outline, using a circular saw. Stop just short of corners, then use a wood chisel to complete the corner cuts. Remove cut siding. Pry remaining siding slightly away from the sheathing around the roof outline to allow for easy installation of the metal flashing. Cover the exposed sheathing with 8"-wide strips of building paper (see step 4, page 90).

11 Set the bay window unit back on the braces and slide it back into the rough opening until the brick moldings are tight against the sheathing. Insert wood shims between the outside end of the metal braces and the seat board (inset). Check the window to make sure it is level, and adjust the shims if necessary.

12 Anchor the window by driving 16d galvanized casing nails through the outside brick molding and into the framing members. Space the nails every 12", and use a nail set to drive the nail heads below the surface of the wood.

13 Drive wood shims into the spaces between the side jambs and the blocking or jack studs, and between the headboard and header. Space the shims every 12". Fill the spaces around the window with loosely packed fiberglass insulation. At each shim location, drive 16d casing nails through the jambs and shims and into the framing members. Cut off the shims flush with the framing members, using a handsaw. Use a nail set to drive the nail heads below the surface of the wood.

14 Staple sheet plastic over the top of the window unit to serve as a vapor barrier. Trim the edges of the plastic around the top of the window with a utility knife.

15 Remove the sheathing pieces from the roof frame, then position the frame on top of the window unit. Attach the roof frame to the window and to the wall at stud locations, using 3" utility screws.

16 Fill the empty space inside the roof frame with loosely packed fiberglass insulation. Screw the sheathing back onto the roof frame.

17 Staple asphalt building paper over the roof sheathing. Make sure each piece overlaps the one below by at least 5".

18 Cut drip edges with metal snips, then attach them around the edge of the roof sheathing, using roofing nails.

(continued next page)

19 Cut and fit a piece of step flashing on each side of the roof unit. Adjust the flashing so it overhangs the drip edge by 1/4". Flashings help guard against moisture damage.

20 Trim the end of the flashing to the same angle as the drip edge. Nail flashing to the sheathing with roofing nails.

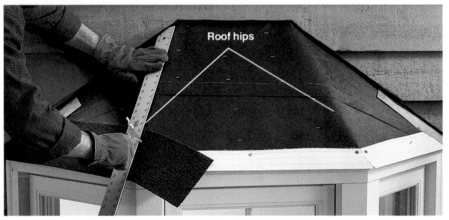

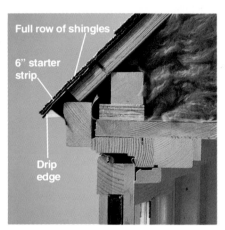

21 Cut a 6"-wide strip of shingles for the starter row. Use roofing nails to attach the starter row so it overhangs the drip edge by about 1/2" (photo, right). Cut the shingles along the roof hips with a straightedge and roofing knife.

22 Nail a full row of shingles over the starter row. Bottom edges should be flush with bottom of the starter row, and notches should not be aligned.

23 Install another piece of step flashing on each side of the roof, overlapping the first piece of flashing by about 5".

24 Cut and install another row of full shingles. Bottom edges should overlap the tops of the notches on previous row by 1/2". Attach the shingles with roofing nails driven just above the notches.

25 Continue installing alternate rows of step flashing and shingles to top of roof. Bend the last pieces of step flashing to fit over the roof hips.

26 When roof sheathing is covered with shingles, install top flashing. Cut and bend the ends over the roof hips, and attach with roofing nails. Attach remaining rows of shingles over the top flashing.

27 Find the height of final rows of shingles by measuring from the top of the roof to a point 1/2" below the top of the notches on the last installed shingle. Trim shingles to this measurement.

28 Attach the final row of shingles with a thick bead of roofing cement, not nails. Press firmly to ensure a good bond.

29 Make ridge caps by cutting shingles into 1-ft. sections. Use a roofing knife to trim off the top corners of each piece, so ridge caps will be narrower at the top than at the bottom.

30 Install the ridge caps over the roof hips, beginning at the bottom of the roof. Trim the bottom ridge caps to match the edges of the roof. Keep the same amount of overlap with each layer.

(continued next page)

31 At the top of the roof hips, use a roofing knife to cut the shingles to fit flush with the wall. Attach the shingles with roofing cement. Do not nail.

32 Staple sheet plastic over the bottom of the window to serve as a vapor barrier. Trim plastic around the bottom of the window with a utility knife.

33 Cut and attach a 2 × 2 skirt frame around the bottom of the bay window, using 3" galvanized utility screws. The skirt frame should be set back about 1" from the edges of the window.

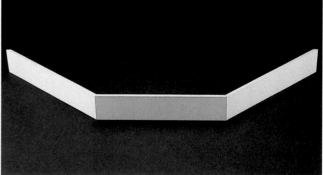

34 Cut skirt boards to match the shape of the bay window bottom, mitering the ends to ensure a tight fit. Test-fit the skirt board pieces to make sure they match the bay window bottom.

35 Cut a 2 × 2 furring strip for each skirt board. Miter the ends to the same angles as the skirt boards. Attach the furring strips to the back of the skirt boards, 1" from the bottom edges, using 2" galvanized utility screws.

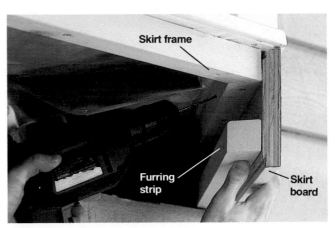

36 Attach the skirt board pieces to the skirt frame. Drill 1/8" pilot holes every 6" through the back of the skirt frame and into the skirt boards, then attach the skirt boards with 2" galvanized utility screws.

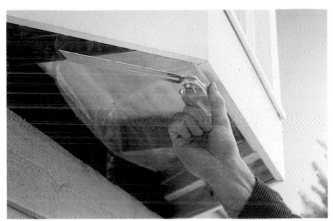

37 Measure the space inside the skirt boards, using a T-bevel to duplicate the angles. Cut a skirt bottom from 3/4" exterior-grade plywood to fit this space.

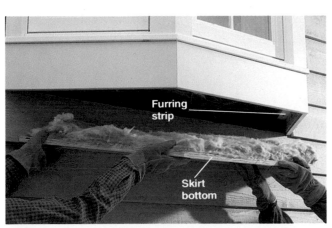

38 Lay fiberglass insulation on the skirt bottom. Position the skirt bottom against the furring strips and attach it by driving 2" galvanized utility screws every 6" through the bottom and into the furring strips.

39 Install any additional trim pieces specified by your window manufacturer (inset), using casing nails. Seal roof edges with roofing cement, and seal around the rest of the window with silicone caulk. Complete the inside finish work (pages 118 to 123).

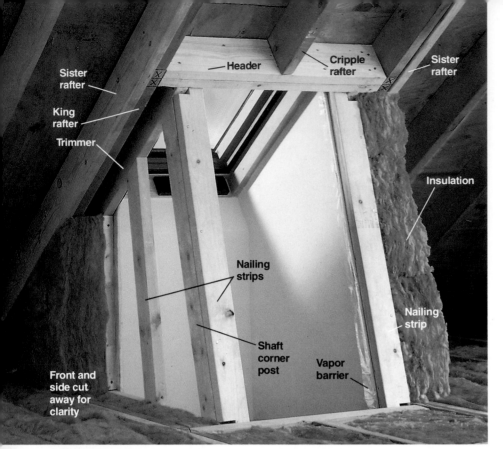

Sister rafter

King rafter

Trimmer

Header

Cripple rafter

Sister rafter

Insulation

Nailing strips

Nailing strip

Shaft corner post

Vapor barrier

Front and side cut away for clarity

A typical skylight installation requires a framed opening in the roof to hold the skylight, another opening in the ceiling, and a framed shaft that joins the two openings. In a home with rafter construction, one or two rafters may be cut to make room for a large skylight, as long as the openings are reinforced with double headers and "sister" framing members. The shaft is made with 2 × 4 lumber and wallboard, and includes a vapor barrier and fiberglass insulation.

Nailing flange

Step flashing

Weatherproof your skylight with metal flashing on all sides. Even if your window has a "self-flashing" mounting flange, it is a good idea to install additional flashings. Flashing kits, available from skylight manufacturers, include step flashings (shown above), a sill flashing to fit the bottom of the window, and a head flashing to fit the top. Sheet-metal shops can fabricate flashings according to your measurements.

Installing a Skylight

A skylight (sometimes called a roof window) is an ideal way to provide additional light and ventilation in areas where standard windows are not practical.

Many homeowners have resisted installing skylights because older models were prone to leakage. But today's skylights, with metal-clad frames and pre-attached flashings, are extremely reliable. When installed correctly, good skylights have the same life-expectancy as windows.

If your roof is supported with trusses (page 13), choose a narrow skylight that fits between the trusses. Roof trusses should never be cut. If your roof is supported with rafters, you can safely cut and remove one or two rafters to frame the skylight opening.

Many people install skylights in direct sunlight, but in warmer climates, it is better to install them on the north side of the roof or in shaded areas.

This section includes:

• Installing a skylight (pages 106 to 109)
• Building a skylight shaft (pages 110 to 113)

Everything You Need:

Tools: tape measure, level, pencil, combination square, reciprocating saw, flat pry bar, miter saw, hammer, ladders, roofing jacks, stapler, roofing knife, caulk gun, metal snips, plumb bob.

Materials: 2" dimension lumber, 10d nails, building paper, roofing cement, skylight flashings, roofing nails, insulation, twine, sheet plastic.

Skylight Shaft Options

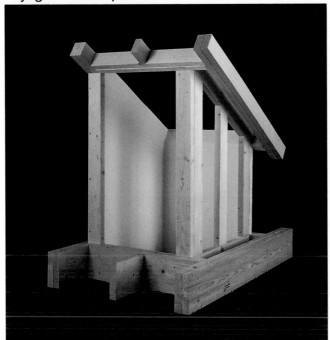

Straight shafts are easy to build, and work well if you prefer soft, diffuse natural lighting. The sides of the light shaft run straight down to the framed ceiling opening.

Angled shafts are longer at the base, allowing a greater amount of direct sunlight into a room. An angled shaft also is more effective for directing light toward a particular area of a room.

Installation Variations

Trusses

No light shaft is required for skylights in finished attics where the ceiling surface is attached directly to rafters. Install the window low enough on the roof to provide a view of the surrounding landscape.

Install several small skylights, instead of one large one, if your home is framed with roof trusses instead of rafters (page 13). Each skylight must fit in the space between the roof trusses. Trusses are critical to the structural strength of the roof, and should never be cut or altered.

How to Install a Skylight

1 Prepare the project area by removing any insulation between the joists or rafters. (In a finished attic, you will need to expose the rafters by removing the interior surfaces (pages 38 to 41).

2 Use the first rafter on each side of the planned rough opening to serve as king rafters. Measure and mark where the double header and double sill will fit against one of the king rafters. Use a carpenter's level to extend the marks across the intermediate rafter to the opposite king rafter.

3 Brace each intermediate rafter by nailing two 2 × 4s between the rafter and the joist below. Braces should be positioned just above the header marks and just below the sill marks.

4 Reinforce each king rafter by attaching a full-length "sister" rafter against the outside edge, using 10d nails. Use a combination square to mark the section of intermediate rafter that will be removed. To accommodate the double header and sill, the removed section of rafter should be 6" longer than the listed rough opening height of the skylight.

5 Remove the intermediate rafter by cutting along the marked lines, using a reciprocating saw. Make an additional cut about 3" inside the first cut, then knock out the small rafter section. Pry out the remaining section of cut rafter with a pry bar.

6 Build a double header and double sill to reach between the king rafters, using 2" dimension lumber that is the same size as the rafters.

7 Install the header and sill, anchoring them to the king rafters and cripple rafters with 10d nails. The ends of the header and sill should be aligned with the marked lines on the king rafters.

8 Measure and mark the rough opening width on the header and sill. For some skylight sizes, this measurement will equal the distance between the king rafters. If the measurement is less than the distance between king rafters, trimmers need to be installed.

9 Cut and install trimmers to complete the skylight frame. Inside edges of trimmers should just touch the rough opening width marks on the header and sill. Avoid installing trimmers by using rafters and joists to frame the opening whenever possible.

10 Remove the 2 × 4 braces supporting the cripple rafters, then mark the rough opening, and cut and remove the roof section as directed on pages 50 to 51.

11 Remove shingles around the rough opening with a flat pry bar, exposing at least 9" of building paper or sheathing on all sides of the roof opening. Remove entire shingles only; do not cut them.

(continued next page)

12 Cut 1-ft.-wide strips of building paper and slide them between the shingles and existing building paper or sheathing. Bend the paper around the framing members and staple it in place.

13 Spread a 5"-wide layer of roofing cement around the rough opening. Insert the skylight in the rough opening so the nailing flange rests tightly against the building paper.

14 Nail through the nailing flange and into the framing members with 2" galvanized roofing nails spaced every 6". (NOTE: If your skylight uses L-shaped brackets instead of a nailing flange, follow the manufacturer's instructions.)

15 Patch in shingles up to the bottom edge of the skylight. Attach the shingles with roofing nails driven just below the adhesive strip. (If necessary, cut the shingles with a roofing knife to make them fit against the bottom of the skylight.)

16 Spread roofing cement on the bottom edge of the sill flashing, then fit the flashing around the bottom of the skylight unit. Attach the flashing by driving 3/4" galvanized nails through the vertical side flanges near the top of the flashing and into the skylight jambs.

17 Spread roofing cement on the bottom of a piece of step flashing, then slide the flashing under the drip edge on one side of the skylight. Step flashing should overlap the sill (bottom) flashing by 5". Press the step flashing down to bond it. Repeat at the opposite side of the skylight.

18 Patch in next row of shingles on each side of the skylight, following the existing shingle pattern. Drive a roofing nail through each shingle and the step flashing, into the sheathing. Drive additional nails just above the notches in the shingles.

19 Continue applying alternate layers of step flashing and shingles, using roofing cement and roofing nails. Each flashing should overlap the preceding flashing by 5".

20 At the top of the skylight, cut and bend the last step flashing on each side, so the vertical flange wraps around the corner of the skylight. Patch in the next row of shingles.

21 Spread roofing cement on the bottom of the head flashing to bond it to the roof. Position the flashing against the top of the skylight so the vertical flange fits under the skylight drip edge, and the horizontal flange fits under the shingles above the skylight.

22 Fill in the remaining shingles, cutting them to fit, if necessary. Attach the shingles with roofing nails driven just above the notches.

23 Apply a complete bead of roofing cement along the joint between the shingles and skylight. Remove roofing jacks and fill nail holes with roofing cement.

How to Build a Skylight Shaft

1 Remove any insulation in the area where the ceiling opening will be located. If there is electrical wiring running through the project area, shut off the power and reroute the circuit before continuing (pages 35 to 36).

2 Using a plumb bob as a guide, mark reference points on the ceiling surface, directly below the inside corners of the skylight frame. If you are installing a straight shaft, these points will mark the corners of the ceiling opening.

Plumb mark

3 If the skylight shaft will be angled, measure from the plumb marks and mark the corners of the ceiling opening. Drive finish nails through the ceiling surface to mark the points.

4 From the room below, mark lines between the finish nails, then remove the ceiling surface (pages 38 to 41).

5 Use one joist on each side of the ceiling opening to serve as king joists. Measure and mark where the double header and double sill will fit against the king joists, and where the outside edge of the header and sill will cross any intermediate joists.

6 If you will be removing a section of an intermediate joist, reinforce the king joists by nailing full-length "sister" joists to the outside edge of the king joists, using 10d nails.

7 Use a combination square to extend cutting lines down the sides of the intermediate joist, then cut out the joist section with a reciprocating saw. Pry the joist loose, being careful not to damage ceiling surface.

8 Build a double header and double sill to span the distance between the king joists, using 2" dimension lumber the same size as the joists.

(continued next page)

9 Install the double header and double sill, anchoring them to the king joists and cripple joists with 10d nails. The inside edges of the header and sill should be aligned with the edge of the ceiling cutout.

10 Complete the ceiling opening by cutting and attaching trimmers, if required, along the sides of the ceiling cutout between the header and sill. Endnail the trimmers to the header and sill with 10d nails.

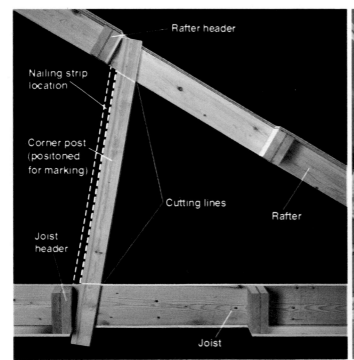

11 Install 2 × 4 corner posts for the skylight shaft. To measure posts, begin with a 2 × 4 that is long enough to reach from the top to the bottom of the shaft. Hold the 2 × 4 against the inside of the framed openings, so it is flush with the top of the rafter header and the bottom of the joist header

(left). Mark cutting lines where the 2 × 4 meets the top of the joist or trimmer, and the bottom of the rafter or trimmer (right). Cut along the lines, then toenail the posts to the top and bottom of the frame with 10d nails.

Nailing strips

12 Attach a 2 × 4 nailing strip to the outside edge of each corner post to provide a surface for attaching wallboard. Ends of nailing strips should be notched to fit around the trimmers, but a perfect fit is not necessary.

Nailing strips

13 Install additional 2 × 4 nailing strips between posts if the distances between corners posts is more than 24". The top ends of the nailing strips should be mitered to fit against the rafter trimmers.

14 Wrap the skylight shaft with fiberglass insulation. Secure the insulation by wrapping twine or duct tape around the shaft and insulation.

Insulation removed for clarity

15 From inside the shaft, staple a plastic vapor barrier over the insulation.

Wallboard and insulation removed for clarity

16 Finish the inside of the shaft using metal corner beads and wallboard (pages 118 to 121). TIP: To reflect light, paint shaft interior with light semi-gloss paint.

Completing the Project

When finishing a remodeling project, strive to make the new work blend in with the rest of your home. A good remodeling project looks like an original part of the home design, not like an afterthought. Wherever possible, use materials and installation techniques that match those found elsewhere in the home.

Because exteriors are exposed to the rain and sun, protect these surfaces by doing the outdoor finishing work first. Patched siding and new trim should be caulked and painted as soon as possible to seal them against the weather.

If your project required one or more work permits, have the building inspector review and approve your work before you close up walls and complete the interior finish work.

Complete all interior work on the walls, including painting or wallcovering, before you attach the trim moldings. If your floors must be patched, do not install baseboard until the patching work is done.

This section shows:

• Finishing the exterior, including exterior moldings (page 115), patching wood lap siding (page 116), and patching stucco (page 117)

• Finishing walls and ceilings (pages 118 to 121)

• Installing trim moldings (pages 122 to 123)

• Patching flooring (pages 124 to 125)

Completing the Project
Finishing the Exterior

For many remodeling projects, the only exterior completion work required is painting and caulking. Some projects, however, require more work. For example, if you have replaced an old door or window with a smaller unit, you will need to patch the exposed wall area to match the surrounding siding. Windows and doors with clad frames require exterior moldings (photo, right).

To patch lap siding, bring a sample of the original siding to your home center and match it as closely as you can. If the match is not perfect, use siding from a hidden area of your house or garage to patch the project area.

To patch stucco walls (page 117), practice first on scrap materials, because duplicating stucco textures takes some skill.

Windows and doors with clad frames have nailing flanges that must be covered with wood or metal moldings, purchased separately. This window was installed in an old door opening, which required patching beneath the window with sheathing, building paper, and siding (see next page).

How to Install Exterior Moldings

1 Cut each molding piece to length, mitering the ends at 45°. Position the molding over the window jamb and against the siding. Drill pilot holes through the molding and sheathing, and into the framing members.

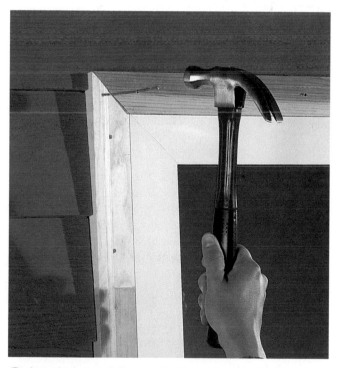

2 Attach the moldings with 8d casing nails. Drive the nails below the wood surface with a nail set. Use silicone caulk to seal around the moldings and to fill nail holes. Paint the moldings as soon as the caulk is dry.

How to Patch Wood Lap Siding

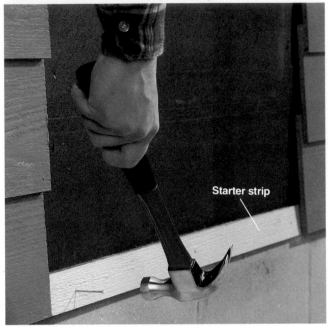

1 Cover the patch area with sheathing and building paper, if not already present. If the bottom row of siding is missing, nail a 1 × 2 starter strip along the bottom of the patch area, using 6d siding nails. Leave a 1/4" gap at each joint in the starter strip to allow for expansion.

2 Use a pry bar to remove lengths of lap siding on both sides of the patch area, creating a staggered pattern. When new siding is installed, the end joints will be offset for a less conspicuous appearance.

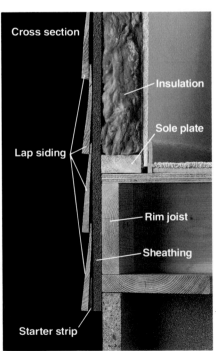

3 Cut the bottom piece of lap siding to span the entire opening, and lay it over the starter strip. Allow a 1/4" expansion gap between board ends. Attach siding with pairs of 6d siding nails driven at each stud location.

4 Cut and install succeeding rows of siding, nailing only near the top of the siding at stud locations. Work upward from the bottom to create the proper overlap.

5 Fill joints between siding pieces with silicone caulk. Repaint the entire wall surface as soon as the caulk dries to protect the new siding against the weather.

How to Patch Stucco

For small jobs, use premixed stucco, available at building centers. For best results, apply the stucco in two or three layers, letting each layer dry completely between applications. Premixed stucco also can be used on larger areas, but it is more expensive than mixing your own ingredients.

1 Cut self-furring metal lath and attach to the sheathing with roofing nails. Pieces of lath should overlap by 2". NOTE: If the patch area goes to the base of the stucco wall, attach metal "stop bead" at the bottom of the opening to prevent the stucco material from leaking out.

2 Mix first stucco coat by combining 3 parts sand, 2 parts portland cement, 1 part masonry cement, and water. Mixture should be just moist enough to hold its shape when squeezed (inset).

3 Use a trowel to apply the first stucco coat in 3/8"-thick layer, directly onto the metal lath. Scratch horizontal grooves into the wet surface of the stucco. Let the stucco set for two days, dampening it every few hours with fine spray to help it cure evenly.

4 Mix and apply a second stucco coat in a smooth layer, so the patch area is within 1/4" of wall surface. Let second coat set for two days, dampening it every few hours. Mix a stucco finish coat made of 1 part lime, 3 parts sand, 6 parts white cement, and water.

5 Dampen the wall, then apply the finish coat to match the old stucco. Practice helps. The finish coat above was dabbed on with a whisk broom, then flattened with a trowel. Keep the finish coat damp for a week, and let it dry for several more days if you plan to paint it.

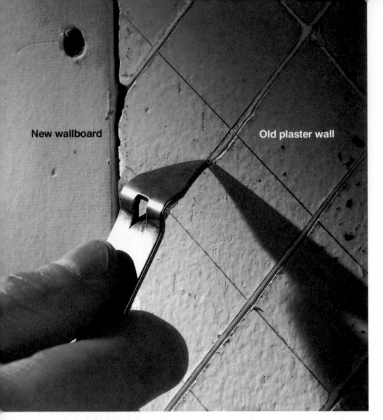

New wallboard

Old plaster wall

Finishing Walls & Ceilings

Use wallboard both to finish new walls and to patch existing wall and ceiling areas exposed during the remodeling project. Wallboard is an ideal base for paint, wallcovering, or paneling.

Openings in smooth plaster walls usually can be patched with wallboard, but if you need to match a textured plaster surface, it is best to hire a plasterer to do the work.

Wallboard is available in 4 × 8 or 4 × 10 sheets, and in 3/8", 1/2", and 5/8" thicknesses. For new walls, 1/2"-thick wallboard is standard.

Use a pointed tool to score old plaster wall surface near patching seams to improve bonding when patching with wallboard and wallboard compound. If the plaster and lath is thicker than the wallboard, you will need to install furring strips on the studs before attaching the wallboard.

Everything You Need:

Tools: wallboard hammer, tape measure, wallboard lifter, utility knife, straightedge, T-square, sawhorses, wallboard saw, cordless jigsaw, wallboard knives, wallboard wet sander.

Materials: wallboard, wallboard nails or screws, wallboard compound, wallboard tape, sandpaper, steel corner bead (inside and outside).

How to Install Wallboard

1 Measure the thickness of the wall surface at the edge of the patch area. Buy new wallboard to match. On plaster walls, include thickness of lath when measuring.

2 Trim any uneven surface edges around the patch area, and make sure framing members have a smooth nailing surface.

3 Where necessary, provide a nailing surface around the edges of the patch area by attaching 2 × 4 nailing strips to the existing framing members.

4 Insulate exterior walls and roof areas by stapling fiberglass insulation to the framing members. The paper backing should face into the house. Staple a plastic vapor barrier over the insulation.

5 Mark the location of the framing members and nailing strips on the floor and ceiling. This will allow you to attach wallboard without relying on a stud finder.

6 Measure the exposed area to find the dimensions for wallboard panels. Joints should fall over studs or nailing strips, but should not be aligned with corners of windows or doors. Leave a gap of no more than 1/4" between wallboard and jambs.

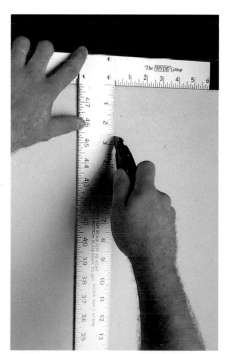

7 Set the wallboard panel on sawhorses with the smooth side facing up. Mark the panel for cutting according to your measurements.

8 To make straight cuts, score the face paper with a utility knife, using a wallboard T-square as a guide, then deepen the cuts.

9 Complete straight cuts by bending the panel away from the scored line until it breaks. Cut through the back paper with a utility knife to separate the pieces.

(continued next page)

10 To cut notches, use a wallboard saw to make the parallel cuts. Score the remaining line with a utility knife, then snap the notched piece backward and cut through the back paper.

11 To make cutouts for receptacles, round-top windows, or other unusual shapes, rub chalk on the outer edges of the object. Press the wallboard against the wall, as in step 12, transferring the chalk to the back of the panel. Remove the panel and cut just outside chalk lines with a jig saw.

12 Position the wallboard panel tightly against the framing members. For large panels, use a wallboard lifter or wood shims to raise the wallboard so it fits snugly against the ceiling.

13 Anchor wallboard panels by driving wallboard screws, spaced every 10", into the framing members. Screw heads should be just below the wallboard surface.

14 At outside corners, cut metal corner bead to length, and attach with wallboard nails, spaced every 8". Apply a double layer of wallboard compound to each side of the corner, using a 6" wallboard knife.

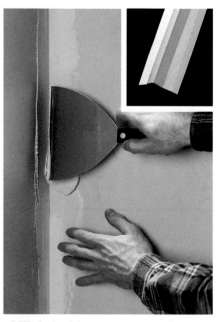

15 At inside corners, apply a thin layer of wallboard compound to each side, using a wallboard knife. Cut inside corner bead (inset) to length, then press it into the corners. Scrape away excess compound.

16 At joints, use a 6" wallboard knife to apply a single layer of wallboard compound to seams and screw heads.

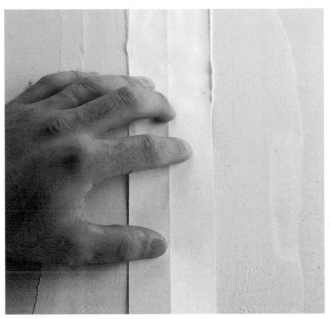

17 Cut a strip of wallboard tape and press it into the wallboard compound at each joint. Smooth the joint with 6" wallboard knife. Cover remaining screw heads with a layer of wallboard compound.

18 Let wallboard compound dry completely, then apply another thin layer to joints, corners, and screw heads, using a 12" wallboard knife. Let compound dry completely.

19 When wallboard compound is dry, use a wallboard wet sander to sand joints smooth. Sander should be damp but not dripping, and should be rinsed frequently.

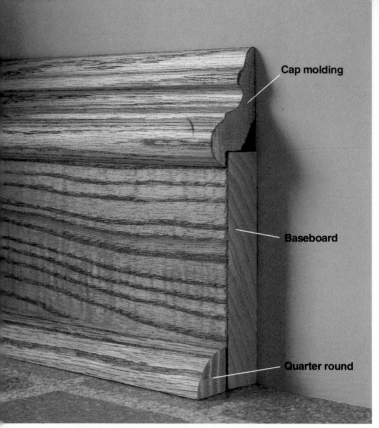

Ornamental trim styles can be created by combining two or more types of standard trim. Molding styles that are no longer produced can be duplicated with this method.

Completing the Project
Installing Trim Moldings

When finishing the trim work on a remodeling project, use moldings that match the style found elsewhere in your home. Home centers sell moldings in many styles, but may not stock the unusual moldings found in older homes.

Many salvage yards carry molding styles no longer manufactured. Or, if you saved trim moldings during your demolition work, use these materials when trimming the new project. Some elaborate molding can be duplicated by combining several different moldings (photo, left).

Wood trim moldings are expensive, so it is a good idea to practice your cutting and fitting techniques on scrap materials.

Everything You Need:

Tools: tape measure, pencil, coping saw, straightedge, miter saw, drill & bits, hammer.

Materials: moldings, finish nails, wood putty.

How To Install Baseboard Molding

1 Outline the profile of the baseboard onto the back of a baseboard section, using a scrap piece of baseboard as a template. Cut along the outline with a coping saw.

2 Fit the coped edge of the baseboard over another section that is butted squarely into the corner of the wall. Drill pilot holes and attach the baseboard with 6d finish nails driven at stud locations.

3 Fit outside corners by cutting the ends of baseboard at opposite 45° miters, using a miter saw. Drill pilot holes and attach baseboards with 6d finishing nails. Drive all nail heads below the wood surface, using a nail set. Fill all the nail holes with wood putty.

How to Install Moldings for Windows & Doors

1 On each jamb, mark a setback line 1/8" from the inside edge. Moldings will be installed flush with these lines. NOTE: On double-hung windows, moldings usually are installed flush with the edge of the jambs, so no setback line is needed.

2 Place a length of molding along one side jamb, flush with the setback line. At the top and bottom of the molding, mark the points where horizontal and vertical setback lines meet. (When working with doors, mark molding at the top only.)

3 Cut the ends of the molding at 45° angles, using a miter saw. Measure and cut the other vertical molding piece, using the same method.

4 Attach the vertical moldings with 4d finish nails driven through the moldings and into the jambs, and with 6d finish nails driven into framing members near the outside edge of the case molding. Drill pilot holes to prevent splitting, and space nails every 12".

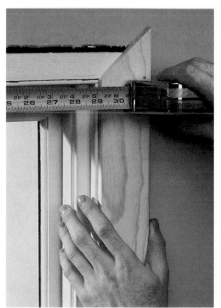

5 Measure between the installed moldings on the setback lines, and cut top and bottom moldings with ends mitered at 45°. If window or door unit is not perfectly square, make test cuts on scrap pieces to find the correct angle for the joints. Drill pilot holes and attach with 4d and 6d finish nails.

6 Lock-nail corner joints by drilling pilot holes and driving a 4d finishing nail through each corner, as shown. Drive all nail heads below the wood surface, using a nail set, then fill the nail holes with wood putty.

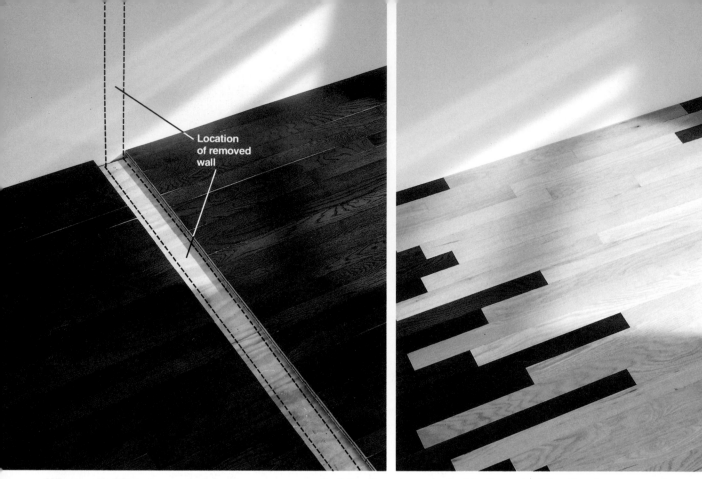

When patching a wood-strip floor, remove all of the floor boards that butt against the flooring gap, using a pry bar, and replace them with boards cut to fit. This may require that you trim the tongues from some tongue-and-groove floorboards. Sand and refinish the entire floor, so the new boards match with the old.

A quick, inexpensive solution is to install T-molding to bridge a gap in a wood strip floor. T-moldings are especially useful when the surrounding boards run parallel to the gap. T-moldings are available in several widths, and can be stained to match the flooring.

Completing the Project
Patching Flooring

When an interior wall or section of wall has been removed during remodeling, you will need to patch gaps in the flooring where the wall was located. There are several options for patching floors, depending on your budget and the level of your do-it-yourself skills.

If the existing flooring shows signs of wear, consider replacing the entire flooring surface. Although it can be expensive, new flooring will completely hide any gaps in the floor, and will provide an elegant finishing touch for your remodeling project.

If you choose to patch the existing flooring, be aware that it is difficult to hide patched areas completely, especially if the flooring uses unique patterns or finishes. A creative solution is to intentionally patch the floor with material that contrasts with the surrounding flooring (page opposite).

How to Use Contrasting Flooring Material

Fill gaps in floors with materials that have a contrasting color and pattern. For wood floors, parquet tiles are an easy and inexpensive choice (above, left). You may need to widen the flooring gap with a circular saw to make room for the contrasting tiles. To enhance the effect, cut away a border strip around the room and fill these areas with the same contrasting flooring material (above, right).

Tips for Patching Floors

Build up the subfloor in the patch area, using layers of thin plywood and building paper, so the new surface will be flush with the surrounding flooring. You may need to experiment with different combinations of plywood and paper to find the right thickness.

Make a vinyl or carpet patch, by laying the patch material over the old flooring, then double-cutting through both layers. When the cut strip of old flooring is removed, the new patch will fit tightly. If flooring material is patterned, make sure the patterns are aligned before you cut.

Install a carpet patch using heat-activated carpet tape and a rented seam iron. Original carpet remnants are ideal for patching. New carpet—even of the same brand, style and color—seldom will match the old carpet exactly.

INDEX

A

Age of house and structure type, 10-11
Aluminum-clad windows and doors, 22
Anatomy of houses, 10-15
Awning window, 20

B

Balloon-framed house,
  anatomy, 11
  framing new door opening, 67, 70-71
  framing window opening, 86-89
  making temporary supports, 52, 55
Baseboard molding, installing, 122
Bathroom,
  code requirements, 17
Bay window, 20
  accessories, 95
  cutaway view, 94
  framing, 95
  installing, 94-103
  supporting, 94, 96-97
Beams, support, 10, 12-13
Bedroom, code requirements, 16, 48

Bow Window, *see:* Bay window
Brickwork and brick facade, 44
Building Codes, *see:* Code requirements

Building Inspectors, *see:* Inspections
Building permits, 24, 30, 34

C

Carpeting, patching, 125
Casement window, 20
  choosing, 19
Case moldings, installing, 123
Caulking, 26, 77, 83, 85, 93, 103
Ceiling,
  height code requirements, 17
  removing section for skylight shaft, 110
Circular saw, 39, 44-45, 47-48, 51, 69-70,
  75, 82, 88, 90, 96, 98
Clad-frame windows and doors, 22
Code requirements, 16-17
Combination windows, 14
Completing remodeling projects, 33,
  114-125
Computer software for remodelers, 24
Concrete block wall,
  anatomy, 48
  removing, 48-49
Concrete floor,
  attaching sole plate for new wall, 64
Connector straps, metal, 17, 62
Connectors, metal framing, 17, 65
Core-block construction, 23
Countersunk lag screws, 61
Cripple rafter, 104, 107
Cripple stud, 14-15, 66-67, 69-70, 86,
  88-89, 96

D

Damp climate, windows for, 20
Demolition, *see:* Removing materials
Disconnecting electrical fixtures, 35-36
Door,
  anatomy of opening, 14, 67
  choosing, 18-19, 21-23, 78
  code requirements, 16
  framing opening, 32, 66-71
  framing options, 15
  installing entry door, 74-77
  installing interior door, 33, 72-73
  installing molding, 123
  installing patio door, 80-85
  installing storm door, 78-79
  prehung, 66, 72-79
  removing old door unit, 31, 42-43
  soundproofing, 21
  styles, 21
  traffic patterns, 18-19
Double-glazed tinted glass, 22
Double-hung window, 20
  removing old units, 43
Double-pane glass, 22
Drip edge,
  around window and door openings, 75,
  82, 91, 99, 108
  types, 91
Drywall, *see:* Wallboard
Ductwork, locating, 35

E

Egress window, 16, 20, 48
Electrical wiring,
  checking for power, 36
  disconnecting, 35-36
Electronic stud finder, 36
Elevation drawings, 24-25
Energy efficiency,
  and doors, 21-23
  and windows, 18, 22
Entry door,
  installing, 74-77
  with sidelights, 21
Exterior surfaces,
  finishing, 115-117
  removing, 32, 44-51, 71
  see also: Lap siding exterior, Masonry
    exterior, Stucco

F

Family room, code requirements, 17
Fiberglass door, 23
Fiberglass insulation,
  for soundproofing, 62
  in remodeled wall, 119
  in window installation, 92, 99, 103, 113
Flashing,
  around bay window roof, 100-101
  around skylight, 104, 108-109
Flooring,
  Patching, 124-125
  Protecting, 37
Framing,
  Balloon framing, 11
  Platform framing, 10
Framing connectors, metal, 17, 65
Framing members, locating, 36
Framing openings, 32
  bay windows, 95
  concrete block, 49
  doors, 66-71
  windows, 86-89
French patio door, 21

G

Gas pipes, locating, 35
Glass types for windows and doors, 22
Glazing options for glass, 22
GlueLam® beams, 57

H

Hall, code requirements, 17
Head flashing,
  around skylights, 104, 109
  at top of bay window roof, 101
Header, 32
  for door opening, 69-70
  for window opening, 86-89, 111-112
  installing permanent header when
    removing wall, 56, 60-61
  materials, 14, 57
  recommended sizes for window
    openings, 14
  temporary support header, 52-55

Hearing protection, 27
Hollow-core door, 21
House structure,
    balloon-framed house anatomy, 11
    platform-framed house anatomy, 10
Hydraulic jacks, 27, 52-54

I

Inspections, 62, 65, 114
Insulation, *see:* Fiberglass insulation
Insulation characteristics,
    doors, 23
    R-values, 22
Interior door,
    hollow-core, 21
    installing, 72-73
    panel, 21
Interior surfaces, removing, 31, 38-41

J

Jack stud, 14-15, 63, 66-71, 86-89, 98
    extra jack stud for bay window, 95
Jig saw, 45, 120
Joint strength, 17
Joist,
    bracing with temporary supports, 52-54
    fastening wall to, 62
    illustration, 12
    king, 111
    metal joist hangers, 17
    sister, 12, 111

K

King joist, 111
King rafter, 104, 106-107
King stud, 14-15, 63, 66-70, 86-89
Kitchen, code requirements, 17

L

Lag screws, countersunk, 61
Laminated beam products, 14, 57
Lap siding exterior, 66
    anatomy, 44
    installing window with masonry clips, 93
    patching after door or window
        installation, 115-116
    removing, 44-45
Lath, removing, 41, 47
Living room, code requirements, 17
Load-bearing wall,
    identifying, 13, 31
    installing permanent header when
        removing wall, 56, 60-61
    making temporary supports, 31, 52-55,
        67, 69
    removing, 10, 14, 31, 56-59
Lockset,
    blocking for, 71, 76
    installing, 73, 77, 85
Low-E glass, 22

M

Masonry anchors, self-tapping, 48-49
Masonry clips, metal,
    for polymer-coated windows, 86, 93
    using on masonry or brick surface, 93
Masonry exterior, 66, 86
    removing concrete block, 48-49
    using masonry clips when installing
        windows, 86, 93
Materials for remodeling, 26
Metal corner bead, 120
Metal framing connectors, 17, 65
Metal lath,
    installing, 117
    removing, 41, 47
Metal siding, installing windows, 90
MicroLam® beams, 56-57, 60
Miter saw, 122-123
Molding,
    for wood strip floor, 124
    installing exterior, 115
    installing interior, 122-123
    removing, 37
Multiple-unit windows, installing, 92

O

Office, code requirements, 17

P

Panel door, 21
Paneling, removing, 38
Parquet floor tiles, 125
Partition wall, 31
    building, 62-65
    illustration, 13
    removing, 31, 56-59
Passive solar collection, 18, 20
Patio door, 21
    installing, 80-84
    tempered glass for, 22
Permits, *see:* Building permits
Picture window, tempered glass for, 22
Planning a project, 10-27
Plans, drawing, 24-25
Plaster,
    anatomy of plaster wall, 40
    patching plaster wall, 118-119
    removing, 40-41
Platform-framed house,
    anatomy, 10
    making temporary supports, 52-54
    new door opening, 67
Plumbing lines, locating, 35
Plumbing pipes, walls for, 67
Polymer-coated wood-frame windows
    and doors, 22, 86
    installing with masonry clips, 86, 93
Post-and-beam saddles, metal, 17
Prehung door, 66,
    installing, 72-79
Preparing work area for remodeling,
    30, 35-37
Project planning, 10-27
Protector plate, 17

R

Rafter,
    cripple, 104, 107
    illustration, 13
    king, 104, 106-107
    removing for skylight installation,
        104, 107
    sister, 104, 106
Reciprocating saw, 27
    using, 41, 43, 45, 47, 59-60, 69-71, 90,
        106, 111
Remodeling ideas, testing, 25
Removing materials,
    exterior surfaces, 32, 44-51
    interior surfaces, 31, 38-41
    old door and window units, 31, 42-43
    walls, 32, 56-59
Ridge caps for shingled roof, 101
Roofing cement, 101, 103, 108-109
Roof, shingled,
    anatomy, 50
    installing on bay window roof, 100-102
    making ridge caps, 101
    removing section, 50-51, 106-107
Roof window, *see:* Skylight
Roofing jacks, 27
    using, 50-51
Room-size recommendations, 17
Roundtop window, 19
    framing opening, 89
    installing, 90-93
R-values of windows and doors, 22

S

Safety equipment for remodeling, 27, 40,
    46, 48, 64
Salvaging materials,
    doors and windows, 42
    siding, 45
    trim moldings,
Sash weights, double-hung windows, 43
Screens,
    Patio door accessory, 80
    see also: storm door
Security, doors, 21
Shaft for skylight,
    building, 110-113
    options, 105
Sheetrock, *see:* wallboard
Shimming,
    bay window, 97-98
    entry door, 76
    interior door, 73
    patio door, 83-84
    window, 92-93
Shingles,
    anatomy of shingled roof, 50
    around skylight, 108-109
    installing on bay-window roof, 100-102
    making ridge caps, 101
    removing section of shingled roof, 50-51,
        106-107
Shingling bay window roof, 100-101
Sidelights and entry doors, 21
Siding,
    anatomy of lap siding wall, 44
    patching, 116
    removing, 44-45

Sill flashing, 104, 108
Single-pane glass, 22
Sister joist, 12, 111
Sister rafter, 104, 106
Skirt for bay window, 94-95, 102-103
Skylight, 20
 building shaft, 110-113
 cutaway view, 104
 installing, 12-13, 104-113
 location, 19
 removing shingled roof section, 50-51
 shaft options, 105
Sliding patio door, 21
 see also: patio door
Sliding window, 20
Solar collector, 18, 20
Soundproofing, 21, 62
Steel entry door, 23
Step flashing,
 around bay window roof, 100-101
 around skylight, 104, 108-109
Storm door, 21
 choosing, 78
 installing, 78-79
Stucco, 66, 86
 anatomy of stucco wall, 46
 patching, 115, 117
 removing, 46-47
 supports for bay window, 96
Stud,
 cripple, 14-15, 66-67, 69-70, 86,
  88-89, 96
 jack, 14-15, 63, 66-71, 86-89, 95, 98
 king, 14-15, 63, 66-70, 86-89
 locating, 36
 making temporary stud wall, 52, 54, 67
 removing, 52, 69-70
Stud driver, 64
Stud ties, metal, 17
Supports, temporary,
 see: Temporary supports
Subfloor, patching, 71

T

Taping wallboard seam, 121
Tempered glass, 22
Temporary supports, 31-32,
 for balloon-framed house, 52
 for platform-framed house, 52-53
 framing a door, 67, 69-70
 framing a window, 87
 making, 52-55
Testing remodeling ideas, 25
Tools for remodeling, 26-27, 64
Traffic patterns, 18-19
Trim molding,
 installing, 122-123
 removing, 37
Trusses,
 fitting skylights between, 104-105
 illustration, 13

U

Uniform Building Code, 16
Utility lines, locating, 35

V

Ventilation of remodeling work area, 37
Vinyl-clad windows and doors, 22, 115
Vinyl flooring, patching, 125
Vinyl siding, installing windows, 90

W

Wall,
 anatomy, 13
 building, 32, 57, 62-65
 fastening to joists, 62
 finishing, 62, 118-121
 removing, 32, 38-41, 56-59
 see also: Load-bearing wall,
  Partition wall
Wallboard,
 anatomy of wallboard wall, 38
 installing, 65, 118-121
 removing, 38-39
Warm climate, window selection, 22
Water supply, shutting off, 36
Whaler, 52, 55
Window,
 anatomy of opening, 15
 choosing, 16, 18-20, 22-23, 104
 code requirements, 16
 egress, 16
 framing opening, 32, 86-89, 95
 framing options, 15, 89
 installing, 33, 90-113
 installing bay window, 94-103
 installing interior molding, 123
 installing skylight, 104-113
 multiple-unit windows, installing, 92
 polymer-coated, 22, 86, 93
 removing old window unit, 31, 42-43
 round-top, 89-93
 styles, 20
 window placement and energy use, 18
Wood flooring, patching, 124-125
Wood lap siding, *see:* Lap siding
Wood lath, removing, 41
Wood paneling, removing, 38
Wood-frame windows and doors, 22
Work area, preparing for remodeling,
 30, 35-37

For Product Information:

If you have difficulty finding any of the following materials featured in this book, call the manufacturers and ask for the name of the nearest sales representatives. The representatives can direct you to local retailers that stock these useful products.

**Bay window accessories
 (page 95)**
Flintwood Products (roof skirt, skirt trim boards, metal braces)
 telephone: 1-800-728-4365

**Computer software for
 remodelers (page 24)**
Expert Software (Home Design)
 telephone: 1-800-759-2562

Metal connectors (page 17)
Kant-Sag (a division of
United Steel Products)
 telephone: 1-800-328-5934

**Manufacturered framing
 members (page 57)**
Trusjoist-MacMillan (MicroLam®)
 telephone: 1-800-338-0515

**Remodeler's blade for
 circular saws (page 27)**
Vermont American Corporation
 telephone: 1-800-742-3869

Storm doors (page 74)
Cole Sewell Corporation
 telephone : 1-800-328-6596

Windows and patio doors
Marvin Windows
 telephone: 1-800-246-5128

Creative Publishing International, Inc. offers a variety of how-to books.
For information write:
 Creative Publishing International, Inc.
 Subscriber Books
 5900 Green Oak Drive
 Minnetonka, MN 55343